Contents

Author's Note

Lack of space and the general plan of the series may have curtailed or prevented the treatment of certain aspects of government in this book: thus topics like education or the influence of British government on practice elsewhere are left mainly to other volumes. Yet even within its modest compass this book could not have been completed without the help of the many persons who have so kindly responded to enquiries and assisted the search for illustrations. Among those who have borne a particularly heavy burden are Mr Maurice Bond, Clerk of the Records in the House of Lords, Mr Frank Cottrill and Miss Sybil McNamee of Winchester City Museums, Mr A. M. Harris of the Public Record Office, Mr J. Hopkins, the Library, Society of Antiquaries, Mr D. F. Petch, curator of the Grosvenor Museum, Chester, and the staff of the National Buildings Record. I am grateful, also, to my colleagues at Leicester University for patience and advice, to the General Editor, Professor Jack Simmons, for encouragement and assistance in generous excess of an editor's duties, and to my wife for her tactful combination of academic expertise and conjugal comfort.

Illustrations

The following abbreviations have been used: B.M. (British Museum), L.C.C. (London County Council, Photograph Library), N.B.R. (National Buildings Record), P.R.O. (Public Record Office), R.C.A.M.S. (Royal Commission on the Ancient Monuments of Scotland), R.T.H.P.L. (Radio Times Hulton Picture Library), S.A. (Society of Antiquaries). All illustrations marked P.R.O. are Crown Copyright, reproduced by permission of the Controller of H.M. Stationery Office.

ILLUSTRATIONS

ILLUSTRATIONS

Medieval Foundations

At her coronation in 1953 Queen Elizabeth II attended at the place where all English coronations have been celebrated in the last 900 years. There she presented herself for the ceremony of Recognition in which survives a vestige of the ancient Teutonic principle of popular election, took the Coronation Oath in a form which, though remodelled in 1689, retains its medieval character, and then, sitting in the venerable chair of King Edward, was solemnly anointed, offered the ring, orb and sceptres—traditional symbols of majesty—and crowned according to a rite that had first received coherent shape in the middle of the tenth century ⟨201⟩. Much of this ceremony may appear an empty, though splendid, pageant: heralds, marshals, champions, noblemen enjoy a few hours of resurrected glory as they stand at the centre of the nation's life; Cabinet Ministers, Members of Parliament, civil servants are relegated to the passive role of spectators, confounded among the black-suited mass of the congregation. An ignorant onlooker would gain from it the most unhelpful ideas about the nature of modern British government. Yet, with all its illusions, it may serve as a suitable symbol of our government, of continuity in the midst of change, of adjustment to the vicissitudes of time without abrupt departure from the traditions of a thousand years. At the least it must remind us that we possess the last of the great medieval monarchies and that the essential institutions and even the unity of the state stand on that common foundation.

The monarch was the most important element in our medieval government. Since the Norman Conquest, at least, he possessed an authority that was in principle and by the standards of the day highly unified and centralised. He derived it partly from his rights as feudal overlord, established at the Norman Conquest, which enabled him to command the allegiance, counsel and services, both military and fiscal, of his vassals; but in time, and as other military resources were developed, the feudal relationship declined into a source of imponderable loyalties rather than real powers, and feudal tenures were valued chiefly for the revenue they produced until their abolition in 1660 ⟨7⟩.

1

GOVERNMENT

Had the king been no more than a feudal overlord the kingdom might have suffered the disintegration that sometimes threatened feudal regimes on the mainland of Europe. He was, however, also a sovereign and sacrosanct. When the king was anointed at his coronation the act was no formality but announced the divine sanction that blessed his authority and set him apart from even his greatest magnates ⟨1, 2, 3, 4⟩. With this ceremony he acquired a sacerdotal character and the right to style himself king by the grace of God (*dei gratia*); and such was the sacredness of his majesty that, until modern times, popular tradition attributed to him the possession of supernatural powers of healing. As a sovereign he could claim that duty to the king took precedence over every other obligation. In establishing feudal services William the Conqueror had been careful not to undermine the sovereign rights possessed by the Old English monarchy. Sub-vassals, paying homage to their lords, had to profess their higher duty to their king, against whom they could not be bound to fight; and this relationship of subject and sovereign was more sharply defined in 1352, when the Statute of Treasons made it treason to levy war against the king, whatever the pretext. The king could summon more than feudal forces: he could raise troops with equal right by means of commissions of array which mobilised men under the ancient defensive obligations of the Anglo-Saxon fyrd. And for his revenues he could draw, in the later Middle Ages, on more than the product of feudal rights and royal estates: the customs, subsidies of tunnage and poundage, and impositions on movable property provided a national system of taxation.

In the centuries following the Norman Conquest the state had developed an intricate and even sophisticated machinery of government. In the past, because government was the personal business of the king, he had to conduct it through his household and personal servants; but, although the household always remained at the centre of government, the expansion of administrative work and the accumulation of written records led, from the twelfth century onwards, to the development of separate institutions for transacting much of the secretarial, financial and judicial business of the crown.

Take the royal secretariat. The writing office of the Anglo-Saxon kings was adopted by the Normans ⟨5⟩, continuing, until the late twelfth century, part of the royal household, served by the clerics of the royal chapel, the only literate servants the king had, and administered by the Chancellor, who was the head of the royal chaplains. The Chancellor acted as the king's secretary, conducted his correspondence and took charge of the Great Seal, with which, in an illiterate age, all royal letters and documents had to be sealed in order to acquire authenticity ⟨9⟩. By the beginning of the thirteenth century this staff had outgrown the confines of

2

the royal chapel and formed a distinct department of state, the Chancery, keeping its own records, the Chancery rolls; and with the multiplication of records it soon ceased to follow the king's person and settled in permanent residence where the Public Record Office now stands in Chancery Lane in London. By its respect for written forms and standardised procedures it introduced a high standard of bureaucratic order into the business of government. Because it kept the Great Seal all the most important and formal acts of state had to pass through the Chancery: treaties, summonses of parliaments, royal grants of land, office, favours and commissions. Because it was the source of all original writs and of many other kinds of writs it also stood at the centre of the judicial system.

As the Chancery established its independence of the household, it lost its immediate and personal contact with the king, and, in consequence, its powers of administrative initiative. In the course of the fourteenth century the Chancery ceased to be the real centre of administration and survived as just a cog, though an impressive cog, in the machine. For while the Great Seal became fettered to the bureaucratic routine of a great office the king began to use his private, or privy, seal for the business of government that required speed and secrecy ⟨10b⟩. This seal had been kept in the household, in the custody of the controller of the wardrobe; but its increasing use now led to the evolution round it of another separate secretarial department, the office of the privy seal. This office superseded the Chancery as the main secretariat through which the orders of king and council were transmitted to the appropriate officials and departments; and its head, the Keeper of the Privy Seal, took his place by the Chancellor and Treasurer as one of the leading servants of the crown.

As the privy seal followed the Great Seal into the grip of a bureaucracy it, too, lost its capacity to serve the king's immediate, personal will; and so, from the late fourteenth century onwards, he began to make frequent use of his signet seal, which was in the charge of his secretary, to issue his immediate, personal commands, either by way of orders to other departments or directly to his officers. The status of the signet was such that when Richard II surrendered to Bolingbroke it was this seal he handed to his captor in token of surrendering his sovereignty. But although the signet acquired a staff and a routine, it never established itself as a separate department, remaining only a small office attached to the household ⟨10a⟩.

The medieval secretariat was a considerable achievement which provided the consistency, co-ordination and record-keeping necessary to good government without entirely sacrificing flexibility; for the king always retained the ability to send immediate warrants to the Chancellor and so cut through the process of signet and privy seal.

The financial administration exhibited a similar complexity. The days were long past since the king used to keep his treasure in a chest under his bed. From the twelfth century his accounts were maintained and audited by the Exchequer, an elaborate institution which had originated, like the Chancery, in the simple arrangements of the royal household and became a separate department as its work required a trained staff and a fixed lodging at Westminster. It took its name from the cloth, chequered like a chess-board, with which the audit table was covered for making calculations with counters ⟨12⟩. The Exchequer early acquired notoriety for the rigour with which it sought to secure the king's fiscal interests; and its procedures were distinguished by the complex precautions taken against fraud, at the cost of much reduplicated effort in book-keeping. It was divided into two sections: the Exchequer of Receipt where money was paid, weighed and assayed, and the sums recorded on the rolls, and the Upper Exchequer where the accounts were audited by an arduous and meticulous inquisition.

Because its procedures were complex and governments always need money, the Exchequer became the largest and one of the most important of the departments. Its head, the Treasurer, formed with the Chancellor and Keeper of the Privy Seal the triumvirate of great royal officers. Its status was such that it was entrusted with a duplicate of the Great Seal, the care of which was confided to the Chancellor of the Exchequer. Its large staff, which, clerks included, numbered forty or fifty, manifested a strong corporate pride and respect for the traditions of the office and were noted for their rigid adherence to the routines it had evolved. Over the centuries it achieved an impressive record of continuity and left a fitting monument of medieval administration in the great collection of pipe rolls, the meticulous, finely written record of accounts, which run in unbroken sequence from the second year of Henry II to the first of William IV, covering a span of nearly 700 years ⟨13, 14⟩.

Administrative elaboration does not always promote efficient government. The Exchequer's long and tenacious memory enabled it to act as a searching guardian of royal rights, but its elephantine procedures and pachydermatous indifference to the promptings of time involved its accounting in years of delay. Its method of book-keeping, to which it adhered with such conservatism that it employed tallies ⟨11⟩ until 1824 and roman numerals until the old office was abolished in 1833, could not produce a realistic statement of the king's finances. Its spirit of routine muffled its response to his pressing needs. The king, therefore, found it at times convenient or even necessary to bypass the Exchequer just as he bypassed the secretarial departments. Within the household there were two departments in particular which, though normally equipped to supply the personal needs of the king and court, could be used for the purposes of government: the chamber, the department of the royal bedchamber; and the wardrobe, the purveying office of the household. When the king required greater speed, efficiency, secrecy and personal control than the routine of the Exchequer allowed, he could turn, as he did during the great wars of the fourteenth and fifteenth centuries, to these more flexible household departments and cut out bureaucratic delays by having revenues assigned directly to them.

Although the secretarial and financial departments performed essential functions, their services were, in a sense, only ancillary to the main activities of government. One of the most important of these was the conduct of war. Warfare remained longer than any other branch of government the personal responsibility of the king. However, because war was an intermittent activity and the king could command nothing like a standing army or navy, no special military or naval department came into being. In the later Middle Ages routine military responsibilities seem to have fallen on a handful of household officers. The most important of these were the master of the horse, the master of the armoury and the master of the ordnance, an office made necessary by the development of gunpowder and cannon: there is also evidence of clerks of the ships. In time of war this staff had to be supplemented from the other resources of the household. Edward III and Henry V, for example, took the wardrobe abroad with them on their expeditions and used it as a field treasury to organise the finance of these campaigns.

By contrast with the conduct of war another of the most important functions of kingship, the administration of justice ⟨15⟩, became to a great extent detached from the king's person. This development followed naturally from one of the greatest achievements of English medieval government, the creation of the common law, that is a law common to the whole country and administered by a centralised judicial system. The volume of business that flowed into the royal *curia*, court or Council, had early led to the separation from it of distinct courts which administered the law in the king's name but without his presence and settled in permanent residence under the great timbers of Westminster Hall ⟨29, 69⟩. By the fifteenth century these courts had acquired most of their mature characteristics. The Court of King's Bench enjoyed the greatest eminence among them because it had maintained the closest association with the royal Council, cases heard before it always being said to be heard before the king himself, and because it exercised jurisdiction in error, where inferior courts had committed errors in procedure: by means of writs like the writ of *mandamus* which commanded the performance of duties neglected, the writ of *prohibition* which forbade the hearing of cases by other courts in excess of their jurisdiction, and the writ of *habeas corpus* which ordered

B

the release of persons wrongfully imprisoned, the Court could superintend the acts of officials and others and secure the supremacy of the law ⟨19⟩. As its name suggests, the Court of Common Pleas, which was the oldest of these common law courts, had jurisdiction over actions between subject and subject: matters of property and debt occupied much of its time and therefore made it, in the Middle Ages at least, the busiest of them ⟨20⟩. The third of these courts was the Court of the Exchequer. It took its name from the financial department in which it originated and continued to concern itself predominantly with revenue cases ⟨21⟩.

A striking feature of this system of royal justice was the degree of independence which the judges soon acquired. Although servants of the king, appointed by him, holding office during his pleasure and administering his law, they had ceased since the thirteenth century to be just civil servants, bound to perform the king's will, and had become judicial experts, chosen from the members of the legal profession that had grown up round the courts. This profession, organised and trained in the Inns of Court, distinguished itself by its sense of corporate loyalty and respect for the traditions and independence of its calling; and under its influence the judges tended to regard themselves as servants of the law rather than executants of the king's will. Nor did they regard the law as the product of that will: they found its basis in the custom of the community, its superstructure in the case-law created over the years by judicial decision; and, in so far as new law had to be made, the only really authoritative instrument they recognised by the fifteenth century was parliamentary statute, the joint act of King, Lords and Commons.

Although the growth of the common law limited the exercise of the king's personal will it marked, at the same time, a great expansion in the power of the crown and the state. For its value lay not only in its independence but in its uniformity. This did not occur in all parts of medieval Europe: France, for example, did not receive a unified system of law until the time of the Revolution and Napoleon. It occurred in England because our kings adopted and were able to enforce a consistent policy from the twelfth century onwards of expanding the business of the royal courts at the expense of the mass of feudal and local courts that had hitherto administered the greater part of civil and criminal justice.

Here the crown owed much to two devices which were to distinguish the English from continental judicial systems—itinerant justices and the jury. Since the twelfth century it had been the practice to send royal officials to hold special judicial sessions in the counties in order to extend the benefits and burdens of royal justice; and by the fifteenth century this practice had developed into more or less the modern system of assize courts and circuits. Regular circuits had been instituted in 1272 by an ordinance

6

which divided the counties into groups and assigned two judges to make the circuit of each group ⟨17, 18⟩.

The assize system did not represent a separate system of law: the judges, by the fifteenth century at least, were drawn from the judicial bench at Westminster, the courts they held were, in effect, local branches of the central courts, the law they administered was the same common law of England. The judges of assize, therefore, helped to assimilate local custom to a national, uniform model.

The institution of the jury was adopted for one reason and continued for exactly the opposite reason. It recommended itself originally by its previous knowledge of the facts of a case: it was only later that it won approval for its ignorance and impartiality. It originated in the device of the *inquest* or inquiry by which the king, in quest of information (as in compiling Domesday Book), sought it from those best placed to give it, the local inhabitants or rather a sworn body of men or jury representing them. Adopted as a means of governmental inquiry, the jury developed in the twelfth century into a means of judicial inquiry. It first proved useful in this way for resolving disputes over property. Its application to criminal cases came a little later and took two forms. The first, the grand jury or jury of presentation, derived directly from the *inquest*: it represented the inhabitants of the shire and had the duty of presenting to the judges any persons whom, either from their own knowledge or from information given them, they suspected of crime. This process of presentation did not of itself establish trial by jury in criminal cases. The trial had to follow; and in the thirteenth century the device of the petty jury was adopted for this purpose. In this second form of the criminal jury the accused was allowed to 'put himself on his country' and have his guilt or innocence determined by 'twelve good and lawful men, neighbours to the place where the fact is supposed to be done'. It was long before trial by jury shook off its association with the *inquest*, before the jury acquired respect because it was assumed to have no previous knowledge of the facts; and the process was not complete before the end of the Middle Ages. Nevertheless the procedure had by then become an essential part of the common law.

By the end of the Middle Ages the common law had acquired unique characteristics which have since impressed themselves on the society and institutions not only of England but of those countries oversea to which Englishmen have taken their legal habits. It had already shown itself a staunch defender of the rights, especially the property rights, of the subject, and the jury was being valued as a protection against improper governmental pressure. Chief Justice Fortescue, when writing in the fifteenth century, contrasted the English system favourably with the French. In France the crown had developed the less archaic and apparently more efficient procedure of inquisition which involved the secret examination of witnesses, torture and presumption of guilt. In Fortescue's view this was the method of absolute monarchy; the processes of the common law and trial by jury were the method appropriate to free men and constitutional government.

Nevertheless, defects afflicted the common law in Fortescue's day and often defeated the ends of justice. Because judges had lost their earlier discretion and adhered closely to precedent and the written word, the law, which had always been predominantly concerned with real property, lost its flexibility and could no longer produce new forms of action to meet the needs of justice in changing social conditions. Procedure was complex, slow and therefore expensive. It was difficult, also, to secure relief from an unjust verdict because the law recognised no proper means of appeal except the limited means of procedure in error.

Means of relief did, however, exist. For one thing there always remained recourse to the king and his Council, for the growth of the professional tribunals had not dispensed him from the obligation to see that his subjects had justice nor deprived him of the prerogative of tempering the rigour of the law with mercy and equity. A more important and accessible remedy lay in the increasing jurisdiction exercised by the Chancellor. As an officer close to the king's confidence, as head of a department responsible for the issue of judicial writs and deeply involved in the administration of the law, as an ecclesiastic versed in the equitable principles of canon law, the Chancellor was well fitted to dispense the royal prerogative of mercy and equity. By the end of the Middle Ages the Court of Chancery had taken shape as a separate court exercising an equitable jurisdiction quite distinct from the common law ⟨22⟩. It attempted to provide relief for those denied justice through corruption, intimidation or mistakes of form: it might intervene where a suitor complained of being too poor to afford the expense of the ordinary course of law; and it occupied itself above all in providing remedies where little or no provision was made by common law, particularly in cases of uses, trusts and contracts. In doing this the Court enjoyed a great advantage over the common law courts through possessing, in the writ *sub poena*, a more formidable means of securing a defendant's presence and, in its summary and written procedure, a speedier means of terminating an action. Yet, in spite of the confidence in Chancery demonstrated by the flow of petitions to it, the activities of this one court and its single judge, the Chancellor, could hardly compensate for the defects of the ordinary law. For all its merits, the English legal system performed its functions imperfectly in the later Middle Ages: it tended to reduce litigation to a battle of wits, tempted men to take the short cut of self-help and often failed to bring the guilty to account.

8

The difficulty of enforcing the law arose also out of another aspect of medieval government, its constitutionalism. The expansion of royal authority and administrative resources does not exhaust the achievements of the medieval period: at the same time there came into being constitutional traditions and practices which were to exert an equally extensive influence on English politics. In theory, at least, the king had never been a despot. In the twelfth century, at his coronation, the king took to issuing a 'charter of liberties', by which he promised to respect traditional law and custom; and in 1215 these liberties received an explicit definition in Magna Carta ⟨8a, 8b⟩. The significance of the numerous reissues and confirmations of the Charter made by King John's successors, which endowed it with the status of a fundamental law, lay, however, less in the particular rights it enumerated than in the general principle it implied, that the king was under the law. This view was strengthened by later constitutional developments and, by the fifteenth century, the common law was imbued with it. Though the king acted in some respects with unfettered discretion, in others he acted only in consultation with the community through his Council and Parliaments.

The king's Council was of supreme importance because it stood at the centre of both politics and administration. It not only advised the king but, when decisions had been made, set the necessary administrative processes into motion by issuing writs and letters under the privy seal. As a tribunal it exercised wide and undefined judicial powers. It took a large part in formulating parliamentary statutes; through the issue of ordinances and proclamations it had a certain legislative power, though not able to override common or statute law. And it frequently performed these functions in the king's absence. The king's personal interest tended to a Council composed partly of personal confidants and officers of the household, partly of the great officers of state, like the Chancellor, Treasurer and Keeper of the Privy Seal. The interest of the community, however, was thought to require the exclusion of members who were mere favourites and the inclusion of others who were sufficiently independent to give honest and impartial advice—the magnates, traditionally regarded as the natural advisers of the king and spokesmen of the community. A wise king might meet this requirement without being pressed, because he could hardly carry the country for long without them; but the conduct of others provoked the attempts frequently made in the fourteenth and fifteenth centuries to exclude favourites and irresponsible advisers by demanding that the king should name his councillors and make them take a public oath to give good advice. It was unfortunate, however, that few of the magnates proved worthy of the part attributed to them; and their attempts to serve the Council and even, during the long minority and personal incapacity of Henry VI, to dominate it, appeared to pervert the constitutionalism of the age to their private profit and seriously weakened the power of government.

The attempt of the magnates to control the royal government by participating in the daily business of the Council was a dubious and, in the long run, an unsuccessful expedient. Parliament, by contrast, appears in retrospect the most fruitful legacy of medieval constitutionalism ⟨28, 30⟩. It was born from the coupling, in the late thirteenth century, of two distinct types of assembly, the one feudal, the other representative and national. The modern House of Lords grew from the one, the House of Commons from the other. At first, only the feudal assembly possessed the name and attributes of Parliament. This assembly developed from the king's court and its origin may be traced to the feudal obligation under which vassals owed aid and counsel to their lord. The king, like any other lord, had the right to summon his chief vassals to his court to sit in judgment or consult with him: these occasions, when his ordinary advisers were reinforced by such prelates and magnates as he chose to invite, were of particular significance because their presence magnified his power and set a more solemn and authoritative seal on his acts. It was to these formal, feudal assemblies or Great Councils that the term Parliament seems to have been applied when it first came into constitutional use towards the middle of the thirteenth century.

The constitutional role of these early Parliaments eludes clear definition. They often served as occasions for giving judgment in difficult cases which the ordinary courts could not decide; and then Parliament would appear in the character of a supreme court of justice—the High Court of Parliament. Sometimes the king chose them as appropriate occasions for the solemn promulgation of laws, so giving Parliament the character of a law-making or, at least, law-registering assembly. He might find it expedient to negotiate exceptional taxation in them, discuss policy, or receive envoys. On the other hand he might do any of these things without consulting a Parliament. Baronial attempts to secure regular and obligatory consultations, though important in enlarging the concept of Parliament's status, were too radical at this time to command general support; and so, at the end of the thirteenth century, the summons, composition and business of Parliaments still remained a matter for the king's discretion.

Parliament, then, began as a particularly formal meeting of the king's court, convened for a variety of purposes: its essence lay in the presence of the king, Council, and such prelates and great men as had been summoned. The process by which a new, representative, element—the Commons—became an essential component of Parliament began in the thirteenth and was not complete until the end of the fourteenth century. The device of representation was already practised in local affairs. The suitors, for example, who attended the shire court were treated as representatives of their localities; and the shire itself was customarily represented, when necessary, at the courts in Westminster by a small number of knights, chosen in the shire court. A means, therefore, lay at hand when the growing importance of the townsmen and smaller landowners made it politic for the government to make closer contact with the local communities.

The first stage in adapting the device of representation to national affairs took the form of the practice, adopted occasionally from the beginning of the thirteenth century, by which the king summoned knights from the shires and burgesses from the towns to treat with him, mostly about taxation. Such meetings, however, were far from forming a House of Commons: the knights and burgesses were not invited at the same time nor to join Parliament, the baronial assembly. The second stage began in the reign of Edward I. Then, for the first time, representatives of the shires and towns were summoned together to a valid Parliament—the Parliament to which Simon de Montfort had summoned them in 1265 being little more than a rally of his supporters. In this stage the Commons—as these representatives of the local communities were to call themselves—had arrived, but only by the skin of their teeth. Their presence was tentative and abnormal. There was no certainty that the knights and burgesses would continue to be summoned, that they would coalesce to form a single 'house', or that they would be the sole representative element.

It was only in the course of the fourteenth century and without design that these uncertainties were resolved. The conflicts between king and barons and the heavy financial burden of the long French wars so enhanced the importance of the Commons that their summons became a regular practice. By force of custom their attendance began to be considered necessary and the Great Council of the magnates, without the Commons, ceased to be accorded the name or attributes of Parliament. In the same period the proctors of the lower clergy, for all practical purposes, stopped attending. From the first the clergy had disliked taking part in a secular assembly, particularly when they were summoned in order to be taxed. This withdrawal of the clergy had important consequences. It lessened the possibility that the prelates might be drawn permanently apart from the temporal barons to form a separate, clerical, estate, and it increased the tendency of the knights and burgesses to be thrown together to form a single 'house' of Commons.

By the fifteenth century the composition of Parliament had become more or less stereotyped. Already certain features distinguished it from otherwise similar assemblies that had arisen elsewhere in Europe. It was not a narrowly professional body of judicial experts, like the French *parlements*. It was not an assembly of estates, divided into several different chambers representing the various orders of society. The House of Lords —to use a term not current until the reign of Henry VIII—did not comprise a single estate, but was a composite body of ecclesiastics and laymen. The lay peers, in spite of having acquired (except in the case of the councillors and judges) an hereditary right to be summoned, did not form a closed caste. The king could still issue a writ of summons to any person he thought fit; he possessed, that is, the right to create new peers and so to alter the composition of the peerage. More important, a peer's right could descend only to one heir; at his death the rest of his family remained commoners. In England, therefore, a numerous, privileged, *noblesse* could not emerge as it did, for example, in France. It also followed from this that the Commons were not divided from the Lords by a deep social gulf. Nor were they sharply divided among themselves. The representatives of the shires, though termed knights, were drawn in fact from a wide social range, stretching from the confines of the peerage at the top to the esquires, lesser gentry and lawyers below; and these, in turn, were not far removed from the representatives of the towns. Neither House, therefore, represented a narrow sectional interest, and there was a large degree of solidarity between the Houses. This may help to explain their success.

It is still difficult to define the scope and role of Parliament. Because the king was an essential component it would be a false antithesis to picture it as fundamentally an impediment to the royal power: it had been called into being to serve the purposes of government and in it the monarchy appeared at its most powerful. It owed its life to the king, for its summons and dismissal was his prerogative (as, in form, it still remains), and there was no certainty about the frequency of its meetings or their length.

The business of Parliaments could now be somewhat more precisely defined. It consisted of four classes: deliberative, judicial, fiscal and legislative. As deliberative assemblies they were important but not essential because there was nothing to require the king to consult them in any particular business. In their capacity as a judicial tribunal they had established themselves beyond doubt as the highest court in the land, but in practice during the fifteenth century they tended increasingly to divert routine judicial business to the professional courts until all that effectively remained to them were the trial of peers and impeachments. In the last two classes of business, however, Parliaments took a fundamental part. There were two things the king could do only in a Parliament: only there could exceptional taxation be authorised or permanent legislation be issued in the form of statute. Without the consent of a Parliament the king could only draw on his customary and personal revenues: he could not repeal statutes and though he and his council could issue ordinances they had no more than a temporary legislative value.

A striking feature of the legislative and fiscal activities of Parliaments in the fifteenth century was the increasing initiative in them shown by the Commons. Much of the proceedings, admittedly, still reminded them that they formed a junior and even an inessential component. Their inferiority appeared (as it does still) in the ceremony of opening a Parliament, when the Lords sat with the Council in the presence of the king while the Commons were kept at a distance standing, cap in hand, at the bar of the House ⟨46⟩; it appeared, too, in its judicial procedure, where the Lords came to occupy the position of judges with the Commons in the part of suitors. Even so the Commons were not just dependent and without initiative. The increasing proportion of petitions addressed to them and their frequent consultations with the Lords, sometimes on better than equal terms, suggest that their assent had become a necessary part of law making. They had established their primacy in granting taxation and it was recognised in the formula by which such grants were made 'by the Commons with the advice and assent of the Lords'. The allocation to them of an habitual meeting-place in the refectory of Westminster Abbey and the regular nomination of one of their number to act as Speaker—a practice apparent from the reign of Richard II onwards—implies an increasing capacity for corporate action. Legislation to secure a regular procedure in elections, such as the statute of 1429 which established the 40s. freehold as the minimum qualification for the county franchise, provides another indication that the importance of the Commons had been recognised and that they had become an integral part of a Parliament.

Although the medieval state had gone far towards creating a united society with a common law, government and representation, this frame of unity embraced a patchwork of communities which enjoyed rights of autonomy in a variety of degrees. The greatest of these autonomous communities was the church, for it enjoyed privileges and immunities which made it a state alongside the state ⟨24⟩. A separate system of government, it exercised jurisdiction not only over the numerous clergy and members of the religious orders but in many respects over the laity. On the one hand the clergy were immune from trial by the king's courts; on the other the church courts had an extensive jurisdiction over the laity in matters concerning tithes, matrimony, probate of wills, and the whole field of personal morality. The clergy were immune, too, from parliamentary taxation and had, in Convocation, their separate representative assembly. Besides this, the church in England owed allegiance not only to the king but to the universal church; a dual allegiance that was most marked in the case of the religious orders with their general chapters and assemblies meeting abroad. Here then was a large sphere of government from which the king's sovereignty was excluded and in which his subjects were exposed to an independent authority. Yet, although the liberties of the church were to be regarded in a later age as an intolerable limitation of royal power, a sufficient *modus vivendi* had been achieved by the fifteenth century to make them acceptable to the king in normal times. In particular he usually got his way over the appointment of bishops; through them he could influence Convocation and obtain grants of clerical taxation parallel to parliamentary grants while observing the formalities of clerical independence.

The privileges of the church provide an extreme example of the innumerable immunities that up and down the country created a variety of exemptions from the ordinary course of administration and established a complicated pattern of local government. At the bottom lay the village, or rather the parish; through it the inhabitants performed their elementary duties, such as those of police, which provided the flimsy basis of public order. Above it stood the old Anglo-Saxon communities of the shire and its subdivision, the hundred, with their courts, jurors and suitors and presided over by royal officials, the sheriff and his subordinate, the bailiff of the hundred. The sheriff provided the link between central and local government. He executed royal writs, empanelled juries, presided over the local courts, took custody of criminals, supervised elections, collected the royal revenue and accounted for it to the Exchequer. The courts of the hundred and the shire had in them the elements of local self-government, in which the freeholders and substantial landowners at least had some part in ordering the life of their community. The sheriff had in him the element of despotism; and had he remained the sole or dominant royal agent he might have become the equivalent of the French *intendant* of a later age. In fact, although both sheriff and shire survived, the part that they took in local government declined in the later Middle Ages. The powers of the hundred and shire courts were sapped by the rise of other jurisdictions, like the assizes. Local government showed an oligarchic tendency, that represented by the justices of the peace. The justices, whose office emerged in the fourteenth century and acquired many of the judicial, administrative and police functions of the sheriff, were not royal officials of the same sort. They exercised official powers by virtue of the king's commission; they could, in theory, be dismissed; but because they were local landowners of some standing they could never be completely dependent agents of the central government. The powers increasingly attributed to them from the fourteenth century onwards thus illustrate an important limit to the monarchy's authority—its inability to create a consistently obedient local

14

bureaucracy and its dependence in local affairs on the co-operation of notables and gentry.

If local administration had been only in the hands of the sheriffs and justices of the peace, its pattern would have been relatively simple. Extensive rights still remained, however, in private or corporate possession, forming franchises enjoyed by prescriptive title or grant from the crown ⟨48⟩. Manors, for example, formed numerous communities within the shire, capable of taking corporate action by means of their manorial courts. Towns enjoyed a similar variety of privileges. Some were sufficiently independent boroughs to be able to exclude the officers of the hundred and the jurisdiction of the hundred court. Other boroughs had been granted by royal charter the status of shires, with right to appoint their own sheriffs and completely exempt from the county administration. (See *The Town* in this series, p. 18.) The universities, too, possessed extensive and highly prized privileges of self-government and even rights of supervision over the towns in which they stood.

In spite of the extent and multiplicity of private and corporate privileges, certain safeguards continued to preserve the rights of the crown. Such privileges could not exclude the judges of assize and could only be exercised within the framework of the common law. Admittedly the palatinates of Chester, Lancaster and Durham provided striking exceptions to this rule; for the king's writ did not run there, the judges of assize had no jurisdiction and administration was vested in a separate hierarchy of courts. Yet, in practice, the consequence of this independence was mitigated. In the fifteenth century Chester and Lancaster were in the hands of the king; and although Durham was ruled by its prince-bishop the king's rights were safeguarded up to a point because he was a royal nominee. Their privileges could not exclude the authority of parliamentary statute; and in practice the system of law and administration in the palatinates was modelled on that of the rest of the country. The chief drawback of these many and varied franchises arose from the administrative impediments they created, such as the rights of sanctuary claimed not only by churches but by many territorial liberties, hampering the enforcement of law and order, making it difficult to bring criminals to account and thus contributing to the lawlessness that characterised the age ⟨25⟩.

It was the misfortune of the Lancastrian kings that this lawlessness extended to the highest ranks of society and undermined the political authority of the crown. The great magnates had always been difficult to discipline. They had their extensive lordships, not so much smaller than the king's, consisting perhaps of a number of honours, reaching into many parts of the country, ruled by an administration which resembled on a smaller scale the royal government. Their influence was not necessarily harmful: inspired by a feudal sense of duty and mutual obligation it could contribute to good government. But in the fifteenth century this influence seems to have been less happily inspired and certainly became more potent. This was a consequence of the great wars with France, for the means used to raise the necessary troops encouraged the magnates to build up private armies of indentured retainers; and with force to back their influence they were tempted to corrupt the course of justice, intimidate the courts in their own or their clients' interests and defy the law. It was impossible to rule the northern borders without the goodwill of Percies and Nevilles; and the lords of the Welsh Marches, whose lands extended into south and central Wales, were able to usurp almost palatine power. In the circumstances of the mid-fifteenth century, when the monarchy was impoverished by wars and the king combined a weak mind with a weak title, royal authority could no longer impose itself on these over-powerful subjects and the conflict of their factions led to the Wars of the Roses, in which it is traditional to see the end of the medieval monarchy.

This unhappy end should not blind us to the achievements of medieval government. During the Wars of the Roses the great departments of state continued to function: the rhythm of the central courts was maintained; and the factions fought to control the government, not dismember or repudiate it. When the wars ended it was possible to restore authority with the old resources; and the old institutions, with some remoulding, continued to provide the basis of government in the following centuries.

In one respect, however, the achievement of the medieval English kings fell short. They secured the unity of England, but not that of the whole island. At the end of the Middle Ages Wales had lost her independence, but had not been fitted into the English political system; Scotland was not only independent but hostile.

*   *   *

Unlike England, Wales did not form a coherent political unit at any time in the Middle Ages, either before or after her conquest. Although her people manifested a strong sense of their common identity, calling themselves indeed the *Cymry* or fellow-countrymen, the bonds that united them were linguistic and cultural rather than political, fostered by bards rather than princes. The attachment of the Welsh to the land of their fathers resembled that of the ancient Greeks—potent to sustain their distinction from other races, compatible with fratricidal strife among themselves.

This disunity need not be attributed solely to Celtic temperament. Their land was unkind to the Welsh. The mountains, while protecting, also divided them; the valleys betrayed them, drawing invaders into the heart

16

of the country. Geography made them difficult to unite, easier to rule from England than Wales. Their social system did not provide the basis of stable government, for the Welsh were not settled agriculturalists or traders, but a pastoral, cattle-rearing people. Their habitations lay widely scattered, native towns arose late and remained few and insignificant. They retained a tribal organisation in which allegiance attached itself to persons rather than places, to kindred or clans and their chiefs rather than to states, and made ordered government on a territorial basis difficult to establish among them.

Such conditions prevented unity. Even within the four main kingdoms into which Wales was traditionally divided the princes found their authority circumscribed by the host of lesser chiefs whose status was almost the equal of their own. From time to time a ruler of outstanding ability arose who secured an ascendancy over his fellow-princes; but this would be a purely personal achievement which could not survive his death. For Welsh custom did not recognise primogeniture and it was therefore difficult to consolidate the authority so gained by transmitting it intact from one generation to another. Thus medieval Wales was racked by endless conflicts both within and between the kingdoms ⟨33⟩.

Disorder and disunity exposed the Welsh to their neighbours, prompted not only by hope of conquest, but by the need to protect the harassed borderlands. Since the days of Alfred and Edward the Elder, English kings had claimed—and sometimes been accorded—suzerainty over the Welsh rulers. The Normans succeeded to these claims and went beyond them; for they encouraged the border earls to engage on a private war of conquest. This was waged with such effect that during the twelfth and thirteenth centuries native rule was eradicated from a great part of north-eastern, central and southern Wales.

This partial conquest nearly served the cause of Welsh independence. By eliminating the other kingdoms or reducing them to the status of clients it enhanced the prestige of the only state that could preserve its independence intact. This was Gwynedd, guarded by Snowdonia, maintained by the resources of Lleyn and Anglesey. There, from the end of the twelfth century, three able rulers in succession tried to take advantage of this opportunity. By encouraging the growth of towns, introducing some elements of feudalism, and securing an undisputed succession to the throne, they attempted to undermine the disruptive influences of tribalism and thus strengthen the state ⟨34⟩. They succeeded so well in this that they seemed on the point of not only uniting what was left of independent Wales but even regaining much of what was lost. Such, at least, was the implication of the treaty of Montgomery, made in 1267 between Henry III and Llywelyn ap Gruffydd, last native ruler of Gwynedd. This

17

agreement granted Llywelyn a great extension of territory and recognised his title as Prince of Wales, with right to the homage of other Welsh rulers and chiefs.

This success came too late. Llywelyn did not have time to consolidate his achievement, which rested on the precarious basis of a disunited England. For England did not remain disunited long enough: indeed the threat of a Welsh revival hastened the understanding between king and barons; and the accession of Edward I put an end to weakness. The king was determined to assert his rights as overlord. In 1277 a brief war demonstrated his strength and reduced Gwynedd to its ancient boundaries. After this it was clear that if Llywelyn was to preserve any sort of independence he must behave with great discretion. But in 1282 a great rebellion forced him to choose between war in support of his fellow-countrymen or ignominious, self-interested inaction. He chose war. It led to his death, the conquest of Gywnedd, and the total extinction of Welsh independence.

The Edwardian settlement did surprisingly little violence to Welsh tradition. It did not affect the whole country, but only the principality of Gwynedd and older crown lands in Wales. Although these territories were now organised in shires on the English model, existing administrative divisions were respected: the Welsh *commote*, the old local unit of justice and finance, survived, for example, under the new name of hundred. English criminal law was introduced—with advantage—but the civil law remained Welsh, apart from the introduction of the jury and system of royal writs. Native rulers and chiefs were displaced by the justices, sheriffs and bailiffs of the conqueror: the great Edwardian castles and their attendant boroughs of English settlers rose in evidence of the country's subjection ⟨35⟩; yet Welshmen continued to serve as lesser officials and the new government was not incompatible with the survival of the Welsh tongue, culture and way of life.

The same is true of the Welsh territories not affected by the Edwardian settlement. These lands, known as the Marches or borderlands, had for the most part been conquered in the eleventh and twelfth centuries and were therefore more anglicised; castles had been built, boroughs established, English and Flemish settlers introduced. But although some parts, like Pembroke, had become quite English in character, in general the pattern of Welsh government had not been drastically altered. The old lordships continued in being, as in many respects the conquerors took over the position of the native chiefs they had displaced, exacting the traditional dues and services, introducing, perhaps, new customs, but not uprooting the old. Outside the boroughs and areas of English settlement Welsh law, custom and language survived.

As far as the structure of government was concerned, then, conquered Wales, though better administered and more peaceful, did not suffer radical change. This was at once the virtue and defect of the Edwardian settlement. It was one thing to respect Welsh tradition, another to preserve, even intensify, the political fragmentation that had been the curse of the country in the past. Edward I had hardly the strength, perhaps not the wish, to overthrow the marcher lordships and so could not give Wales unity or uniformity. Even the lands directly administered by the crown were divided into three parts. The county of Flint was made dependent on Cheshire. Anglesey, Caernarvon and Merioneth—formed from the territory of Gwynedd—were governed from the castle of Caernarvon where an exchequer was established and an officer known as the justice of north Wales represented the king. Cardigan and Carmarthen had a separate administration with its own exchequer and under a justice of west Wales. These territories, then, though known collectively as the Principality and, after 1301, placed under the titular rule of the king's eldest son, did not form a closely integrated unit. Yet the Principality seemed a model of coherence in comparison with the patchwork of marcher lordships between which more than half the country continued to be divided. Here nothing was changed. They were not organised into shires, nor subordinated to royal sheriffs, nor subjected to the jurisdiction of the English courts. The Marches remained, in effect, in the hands of a large number of semi-independent rulers.

In the later Middle Ages Wales lay in a limbo, neither free nor assimilated into England. The near-anarchy of the Welsh Marches hurt the English as much as the Welsh. It was not merely that the border itself was insecure but the government of the whole country was infected with its violence. Much of the disorder that marked the fifteenth century had its origin in Wales. Many English magnates drew their power—and their feuds—from their Welsh estates. It was, for example, the accession of the house of York to the numerous marcher lordships accumulated by the Mortimers that enabled them to challenge the Lancastrians for the throne. Large numbers of Welsh soldiers fought on both sides in the Wars of the Roses, and in the last battle Henry VII won his victory under the dragon standard of Cadwallader. In this fashion the Welsh repaid their conquerors.

*　　*　　*

The Scots succeeded where the Welsh failed in the Middle Ages: they secured unity and preserved their independence. This achievement appears a triumph of art over nature, a tribute to the power of government. The early Scottish rulers had to overcome the impediments presented by a mountainous land and tribal organisation, such as had thwarted the Welsh; and they lacked the basis of an underlying racial and cultural unity on which to build. They had to create a country from a congeries of different races: Gaelic Scots and Picts in Scotia, Norsemen in the Isles and the north, English in Lothian in the south-east, Britons in Strath-clyde in the south, and more Gaels in the south-western peninsula of Galloway; and to these were added in the twelfth century Flemish immi-grants to the towns and French-speaking Anglo-Normans. Even the border that was eventually defined between Scotland and England was an artificial creation in the sense that it cut across the ancient kingdoms of Cumbria and Northumbria and divided the Britons and English of Strathclyde and Lothian from the peoples of northern England with whom they shared a common speech, origin and tradition. On the other hand the Scots enjoyed advantages denied the Welsh. Their country, unlike Wales, had a natural centre between the Tay, Forth and Clyde, from which it was possible to dominate both north and south. More im-portant, Scotland lay farther than Wales from the centre of English power and, whereas the Welsh were hard pressed almost from the moment the Normans conquered England, the Scots were not seriously challenged until the end of the thirteenth century. When the challenge came their sense of community was sufficiently consolidated to withstand the shock.

By this time Scotland had been united for at least two centuries. The kings of Scotia, who had their seat at Scone, pushed their power south-wards during the eleventh century and by the end of the reign of Malcolm Canmore, who died in 1093, had established their supremacy over Lothian, northern Strathclyde and Galloway. The kingdom, however, lacked co-hesion, being little more than a loose union of almost independent regions. To consolidate their power the successors of Malcolm had to shake off their native traditions and adopt the methods that gave the English monarchy its strength. They were themselves anglicised to some extent, allied by marriage to the English royal house, and, as earls of Huntingdon, possessed large English estates which gave them a close acquaintance with the methods and personnel of Anglo-Norman administration ⟨38, 39⟩. In the reign of David I and his successors in the twelfth and thirteenth centuries the government of Scotland was moulded to a great extent on the model of England. Hitherto the course of the succession, determined by Gaelic custom, had led, as in Wales, to disputes and contests that kept the monarchy weak: now the Scottish kings secured the recognition of the alien, feudal principle of primogeniture, a source of stability and strength. Feudal relationships took the place, as far as possible, of the precarious tribal ties: Anglo-Norman barons, many from the Huntingdon estates, had fiefs created for them in Scotland; and the native nobility were

20

gradually feudalised. The ritual of a feudal court magnified the ruler's majesty.

At the same time the disruptive tendencies of feudalism were balanced by attempts to create a centralised administration. As in England, the royal household provided the mainspring of government, with the great officers like the Chancellor and Chamberlain (or Treasurer) controlling administrative departments and supplying the permanent nucleus of the king's Council. The Chancery, which had custody of the king's seal, itself based on the Great Seal of England, acted as the central agency transmitting royal orders by means of writs closely modelled in form and language on those issued by the English Chancery. The Chancery and Exchequer kept in close touch with local administration through the newly created sheriffdoms and their sheriffs, who, like their English counterparts, had both judicial and fiscal functions. A common law was slowly imposed on the varied customs of the regions that composed the kingdom. The revenues of the crown were increased by the foundation of chartered towns or burghs with trading monopolies and rights of self-government. Even the reorganisation of the Scottish church served the purposes of the crown. By introducing a regular parochial system, dividing the country into dioceses with clearly defined boundaries, and securing from the papacy a bull which declared that the Scottish church was completely independent of England, the Scottish kings nourished a sense of corporate unity that communicated itself from the clergy to the laity and contributed to the cohesion of the state.

By the end of the thirteenth century Scotland, though still poor and weak, had been transformed. No longer an ill-defined and ill-organised tribal area lying on the Celtic fringe of Europe, the country now stood within the pale of medieval civilisation, a viable feudal state. It might have seemed that this achievement had been secured at the price of eliminating from its government the features that were particularly Scottish and preparing the way for the eventual assimilation of Scotland to England; but the crisis that arose in 1290, when the child-queen Margaret died and left the succession in dispute, turned the two countries into bitter enemies and put off the possibility of union for centuries.

When Edward I used the crisis as a means of securing the suzerainty he claimed over Scotland he provoked into active consciousness the sense of national identity and unity that had been fostered unawares by two centuries of administrative unity. The result was the long war of independence, which set the countries on divergent paths so that, when the Union at last came about in 1707, the differences between them—in government at least—were much more marked than they had been in 1290: the institutions of Scotland had become recognisably Scottish ⟨40, 41⟩.

GOVERNMENT

In some respects in the later Middle Ages the experience of Scotland did not differ greatly from that of England—a weakened monarchy, a war-like and restless nobility, disorder and disrespect for law, constitutional growth. But in Scotland the troubles, though stopping short of prolonged civil war, lasted longer and went deeper. The great nobles were more independent than their English counterparts, the power of the baronial courts being less eroded by the growth of royal courts and the scope of royal justice more drastically limited by grants of 'regality', a right which invested the recipient and his heirs with quasi-regal powers over the area of his jurisdiction and almost completely exempted it from the interference of the king's officers. Royal authority was also subverted by the practice of forming leagues or bands of 'manrent', by which a great man would attach to himself a following of clients and retainers bound to sustain one another's cause, even against the law. In these conditions the Scottish kings were engaged in a ceaseless struggle with their nobles; and they were handicapped in this by their extraordinary capacity for getting themselves killed in their prime and leaving the country to endure the perils of pro-longed regencies. An able king, like James I, who had the will to govern, could still find the power. James II, assuming his rights after an eleven years' minority, overthrew the mighty 'Black' Douglases and annexed their vast estates; and at the end of the fifteenth century James IV en-forced royal authority over the Western Isles, which had hitherto enjoyed an almost complete independence. Yet each of these was a personal achievement which could not be consolidated; and in each subsequent minority the authority of the crown again sank in a storm of violence ⟨43⟩.

As in England, the conflicts between king and nobility and the needs of the crown stimulated the development of Parliament. The Scottish Parlia-ment began, like the English, as a feudal assembly, a formal meeting of the king's court at which the royal Council was reinforced by the atten-dance of his vassals; and, like the English also, it had functions that de-fied exact definition, being a court of justice and a law-declaring, tax-granting and consultative assembly. In the fourteenth century it became at times a considerable constitutional restraint on the crown, particularly when the burden of ransoming David II—captured by the English—made necessary exceptionally heavy taxation, extended over a long period. At the same time these financial needs led to the summons of representatives of the Commons.

At this point, however, the Scottish Parliament developed in a different way from the English. Its members continued to meet in a single chamber: no separate House of Commons emerged. For the Commons consisted only of burgesses and, as the burghs—or at least the royal burghs—had the status of vassals-in-chief, their representatives could with propriety

22

sit with the Lords. It was not until 1428 that an attempt was made to summon representatives of the lesser landed proprietors, when James I tried to create a Commons on the English model; but they failed to attend, being perhaps too dependent or too poor to afford it.

The failure to create a widely representative House of Commons helps to explain why in Scotland Parliament did not play so great a part in national life as in England. The burgesses represented a particularly narrow section of society: the burghs were set apart from the countryside by law and privilege and stood always in the defensive posture of colonists in an alien and hostile land. It was this narrow sectional interest that they were principally concerned to serve in Parliament. Indeed it became the practice for them to meet separately and beforehand to consider how best to serve that interest; and these meetings, which in the sixteenth century took formal shape as the Convention of Royal Burghs, made it seem that the burgesses were rather delegates of the burghal governments than representatives of the country.

Parliament, then, remained a predominantly feudal assembly. But even in this form it did not achieve the constitutional importance of the English Parliament. Because taxation was rarer in Scotland its financial powers had less political effect. Because members were reluctant to attend long sessions, devices were adopted to speed its business; and these undermined its independence. One such device was to devolve the full powers of Parliament on to a commission elected from its members, leaving the rest free to go home. Another was to appoint a few members to prepare the business to be set before Parliament, particularly to draft the text or 'articles' of proposed legislation. The danger of employing this device of a 'Committee of the Articles', which became a regular practice after 1467, lay in its tendency to put the real power of decision in the hands of a small group and to leave Parliament as little more than a registering agency. In practice these devices could serve the purposes of either baronial faction or a determined king; and their use made Parliament the tool of one or the other.

Scotland had to pay a high price for independence. The promise of the early Middle Ages was not fulfilled and men looked back to the thirteenth century as a golden age, from which their country had since declined. The process of integration had lost momentum, royal justice ceased to advance. It was not only that regalities and other private jurisdictions continued to flourish, but even the sheriffs' courts, which remained the most important instruments of local justice, tended to fall into private hands, as it became the practice to grant hereditary sheriffships to members of the baronage. And the power of the sheriff was not balanced by the rise of new officers, like the English justices of the peace, or tempered by assize judges on circuit. At a time when in England the legal profession was developing the common law into a subtle and complex instrument, Scottish law marked time, ceasing to borrow from England, not yet turning for inspiration to the Continent. In the long run this hiatus may have served Scotland well, for it created few obstacles to the rational development of the law in later centuries; but at the time it aggravated the defects of the courts and contributed to the lack of justice of which such frequent complaints were made in the later Middle Ages.

Scottish independence also proved costly to the English. The hatred between the two peoples not only threatened England with a stab in the back when engaged in foreign war, but kept the border in turmoil. At best the rough inhabitants of these remote moors and dales were difficult to police, with little respect for authority, English or Scottish; and endless disputes could arise over the demarcation of the border: but as long as the two countries remained at peace some sort of order could be imposed. During the thirteenth century an effort had been made to establish an agreed frontier and on either side of it three administrative zones had eventually been created, known as the East, West and Middle Marches. Each March was administered by a lord warden, who had the duty of resisting invasion, keeping the peace, and preventing smuggling, particularly of horses and cattle. Each warden kept his court, where he administered border law; and a joint court, held on the border by the English and Scottish wardens, determined disputes between the borderers of both countries. However, during the next two centuries and beyond, when war or threat of war disturbed the whole region, these measures of pacification could not prevail. The border remained the least civilised and most martial region of England and as wild as any in Scotland ⟨44⟩. Its defence excused—on both sides—the military power of great families, like the Percies and Cliffords, Douglases and Homes, with their host of lesser followers. Ruling their lands like petty kings, the border lords proved as turbulent and dangerous to their kings as those of the Welsh Marches. Their feuds, similarly, infected the whole country, so that, as long as England and Scotland were at odds, the state of the border menaced the good government of both kingdoms. Here, then, was one of the great failures of medieval statesmanship in Britain, a failure which undermined the solid results achieved in other spheres of government.

Revolution and Compromise

'It is manifestly declared and expressed that this realm of England is an empire . . . governed by one supreme head and King . . . furnished by the goodness and sufference of Almighty God with plenary, whole and entire power . . . to render and yield justice and final determination to all manner of folk resiants [residents] or subjects within this realm . . . without restraint or provocation to any foreign princes or potentates of the world.'

THESE WORDS, TAKEN FROM THE PREAMBLE TO HENRY VIII'S Act of Appeals, with their proud assertion of the sovereign independence and self-sufficiency of the English realm, express the temper of a new age. Hitherto, for all its individuality, England had been a characteristic product of western Christendom. Its government was not unique, but only a variant of a common type; parliaments, for example, had proliferated in the later Middle Ages and the English version did not necessarily appear at the time the most developed or strongest. After the fifteenth century, however, this relationship changed. Insulated to some extent from the pressures that moulded continental governments, able to survive without recourse to the large standing armies that proved necessary abroad and to endure disagreement without disaster, England had gone its own way, to emerge with a political system so distinctive that when in the eighteenth century the French writer Montesquieu came to describe it for his fellow-countrymen he felt bound to spell out its fundamental principles as if mapping an unknown territory.

England was not immune from the tendencies of the mainland. Politics here moved to a similar rhythm—the first phase marked by the tendency to absolute, centralised monarchy; the second by political discord and constitutional crisis; the third by relative harmony, arising from tacit agreement between monarch and aristocracy—but at a different pace and intensity which gave the English experience a unique character.

*   *   *

GOVERNMENT

The first phase coincides more or less with the rule of the Tudor dynasty. Under their masterful government the sovereignty of the state was personified in the majesty and supremacy of the king. More than ever he set himself apart from his subjects by the regal splendour and courtly ceremony that this family deliberately cultivated and the age demanded ⟨46, 70⟩. The king stood out the more because the military power of the magnates was drastically diminished. In the seventeenth century the old allegiances still survived strongly enough to enable the Earl of Newcastle in the north or the Marquess of Worcester in the Welsh Marches to raise substantial armies for the Civil War; but the last baronial rising of the old sort had been the rebellion of the northern earls in 1569 and it had proved a short and miserable fiasco. In general under the Tudors English swords grew rusty; and the crown shone more splendidly by contrast.

The Tudors pushed forward the process of national consolidation that had languished since the thirteenth century; and in doing so served themselves. They consolidated the realm and their personal ascendancy at the same time. Feudal franchises were reduced to insignificance and the reach of the common law extended by an Act of 1536 which assimilated the practices of such liberties to those of ordinary counties: although the ancient palatine courts of Durham and Lancaster survived, ultimate control now clearly lay with the king's courts. Even the greatest of feudal franchises—the church—was subordinated to the crown. Hitherto, in spite of the influence the king had enjoyed over the hierarchy, the church had remained an autonomous community. In utterly destroying papal authority in England and establishing a royal supremacy in its place the legislation of Henry VIII and Elizabeth carried through a political revolution of the first order ⟨47, 49⟩. The great system of ecclesiastical courts retained its jurisdiction over laity as well as clergy. But the church was brought within the power of the state personified in the monarch: although the forms of election continued to be observed the archbishops and bishops were in future named by the king: prayer-book, doctrine, even the definition of heresy, were determined by the state; and the church was forbidden to legislate for itself without royal consent. After the monastic orders had been dissolved, the heads of religious houses ceased to sit in Parliament; and, with the confiscation of monastic property and whittling away of other clerical estates, the higher clergy, at least, lost something of their former social and economic status. The Church in England became the Church of England and the old condominium gave way to the claims of the unitary state.

The Tudors also carried forward the process of unification by securing the union of Wales with England and eliminating the marcher lordships. Possessing not only the Principality but the great Welsh estates of the

26

Lancastrians and Yorkists, they had the power to undertake the thorough reorganisation that Edward I had not attempted. Statutes of 1536 and 1543 gave Wales for the first time a uniform administration, abolished both the old Principality and the marcher franchises, and organised the whole country into twelve shires on the English model. This incorporation into the English state was completed by the grant of representation in the English Parliament.

Welsh patriots have sometimes charged the Tudors with sacrificing by this union the true interests of their race. It had the effect, the allegation goes, of anglicising the Welsh gentry, alienating them from their native culture, and depriving the people of their natural leaders. This charge seems difficult to sustain: the process undoubtedly took place, but as the result less of these purely administrative changes than of economic and social causes which the Tudors could hardly have controlled, even had they wished. It would be more just to dwell on the merits of this legislation and the care taken to respect Welsh interests. For, although the courts were to administer the English common law, provision was made for accepting native law and custom where possible; and, furthermore, to avoid the hardship of undue centralisation, although supreme jurisdiction rested with the courts at Westminster and Parliament, the normal administration of law was confided to special courts, known as the Courts of Great Sessions, which were held in Wales, perambulated the country, and performed the functions of king's bench, common pleas and assizes. Most striking of all was the trust—considered foolhardy at the time by some responsible Englishmen—shown by the Tudors in appointing Welshmen to administrative posts and, in particular, as justices of the peace. If the Welsh were not exactly led to paradise they were at least rescued from the limbo in which the Middle Ages had left them. The Tudors contributed more to the good government and civilisation of Wales than any rulers since the Romans.

The Tudors not only consolidated the English state by securing recognition of a common and uniform sovereignty: they also extended the scope and responsibilities of government. They had to establish standards of religious conformity, compel attendance at church, impose penalties on Roman Catholic and Protestant dissenters. The introduction of printing greatly enlarged the bounds and impact of controversy and made it necessary to control the press. The system of regulation finally established in 1586 forbade printers to set up anywhere except in London, Oxford and Cambridge, required them to be registered with the Stationers' Company, who were empowered to search for prohibited books, and made it an offence to publish anything that had not been officially approved ⟨59⟩.

Tudor governments also enlarged their control over the economy.

GOVERNMENT

Regulation of trade and industry was not novel in principle, for medieval rulers had standardised weights and measures ⟨54⟩, fixed wages and attempted to control imports and exports. What was new was the scale on which the government acted to preserve social stability ⟨53⟩ and encourage trade in face of the economic storms that blew across Europe during the second half of the sixteenth century. Monopolies to trade in certain regions overseas were granted to chartered companies, of which the East India Company was the most illustrious. Shipping and seamanship were encouraged by introducing compulsory fish-eating days ⟨52⟩. At home, by granting monopolies to companies or private persons, the government tried indirectly to regulate a wide range of trades and industries such as iron, coal, salt, munitions, leather, starch, beer and wine; and, although in practice these monopolies for the most part did more harm than good, their extent well illustrates how broadly the right of intervention was interpreted ⟨73⟩.

At its most ambitious this right amounted to nothing less than a claim to determine the very structure of society, at least at its lower levels. This is very evident in the Statute of Artificers of 1563, which established a comprehensive code to regulate the employment of the labouring classes. It tried to restrict the mobility of labour by forbidding men to move from the places or occupations into which they were born and enforcing the requirements of apprenticeship in trades. It empowered the justices to compel able-bodied but idle persons to work, if men in agriculture, if women in domestic service; and, in further pursuit of the idle, set a working day for labourers that extended—with two and a half hours for meals—from five in the morning to seven or eight at night from mid-March to mid-September and from dawn to dusk in winter.

The Statute of Artificers aimed further than the resources of the state could then reach, and the Tudors' powers of government were exercised to much greater effect in their treatment of the poor. The Elizabethan poor law, codified by the Acts of 1597 and 1601, exemplified several characteristics of the social legislation of this period: it was the product of long experience and experiment; it applied on a national scale methods already devised by a number of local authorities, and it acted as much as a measure of police as of welfare. For in these disturbed times, when the forces of public order were weak, the swarms of beggars and vagrants, about whom there were so many complaints, presented a threat to good government. Hence the new code bore a double aspect. On the able-bodied beggar, who could work, but—it was thought—would not, it imposed harsh penalties of whipping and branding. For the genuine unemployed it provided work; for the young, the aged and helpless, relief. It made each parish responsible for its poor, for apprenticing their children, providing materials for

28

employment, raising funds by a compulsory poor-rate. It says much for the quality of Tudor government that it not only tackled a problem which France, for example, continued to treat as purely a subject for ecclesiastical charity, but produced a solution which served its purpose for over two centuries and secured the co-operation of the propertied classes who had to foot the bill ⟨57⟩.

The poor law, which substituted a uniform, national policy for the local efforts of scattered towns, illustrates the transition from the medieval to the modern state. Yet the apparatus of government remained in many respects medieval. It was still the king's personal responsibility to govern: the dissensions of Edward VI's reign revealed the dangers that might arise when, because the king was a minor, that responsibility could not be exercised. And the Council remained the chief agent of the king's government. In the composition of their Council the Tudors in general achieved what was probably the ideal of many medieval kings, a body restricted to the smallest and most intimate circle of royal officers and advisers. The Privy Council, as it was called after the reign of Henry VIII, consisted usually of between twelve and eighteen members. Small as it was, its meetings were not always fully attended, for the Council had to follow the ruler; and much of the routine work fell on the handful of constant attenders. To cope with the pressure of business they had to adopt businesslike methods, keeping—after 1540—a register or minutes, holding regular meetings, employing a staff of clerks, ushers and messengers.

The activities of the Council became more multifarious as the state's functions grew, and no more easy to define. It could do anything it thought necessary, as long as it remained within the law. It gave orders about the greatest and smallest matters of state; nothing was too big or too trivial for its attention. It organised the kingdom's defences; it ordered the king's tailor to make night-clothes for a prisoner in the Tower and specified the cost with the care of a housewife. It not only administered the country, often in detail: its functions also verged on the judicial. Because it was responsible for the security of the state it investigated conspiracies, examined witnesses ⟨58⟩, held suspects and, if necessary, committed them for trial. Because it was close to the king, who still appeared as the fount of justice, it also exercised something like a civil jurisdiction, in that private suitors would address themselves to it, hoping for a speedy remedy.

The Privy Council, then, stood at the very centre of administration, a handful of men providing the impulse of royal government. In this respect it did not greatly differ from the medieval Council; but the Tudors developed the machinery of conciliar government by evolving or creating the so-called conciliar courts, which may be regarded as offshoots of the Council, taking over some of its burdens.

Most important of these was the Court of Star Chamber. Because it drew its authority from the ancient jurisdiction of the Council and did not require the sanction of statute it came into being almost unnoticed and its origins remain obscure. It seems to have arisen from regular meetings of the Council, held in a particular place—the Star Chamber at Westminster—and for a particular purpose, to secure law and order. By the middle of the sixteenth century these meetings had become distinct from those of the Privy Council; and it was then possible to speak of Star Chamber as a court in its own right. Even so, it retained a close connexion with the administration because its most important members were themselves Privy Councillors. Above all it had the function of securing the king's peace and respect for the law. Anything that might lead to a breach of the peace—riot, assault, forcible entry, even libel and slander—came within its jurisdiction. It particularly concerned itself with stamping out abuses which undermined the administration of justice. It enforced royal proclamations; and by this means acquired a number of miscellaneous functions, such as the regulation of the press ⟨59⟩. It gained a flourishing business in private litigation. Star Chamber, then, was a formidable and also popular court, a potent instrument of order and an efficient source of redress.

The Tudors' concern for order led them to create conciliar jurisdictions of another sort, offshoots of the central Council planted in the provinces where distance from London and a record of lawlessness created special difficulties of government. Most important of these was the Council of the North, designed to control the most turbulent region of England where the problems associated with poverty, feuds, over-mighty magnates and feudal liberties were exaggerated by its situation as a frontier province responsible for defence against hostile Scots.

Although founded by Richard III the Council of the North did not become a regular and continuous institution until after 1536 when the northern rebellion known as the Pilgrimage of Grace forced Henry VIII to set it on a permanent footing. He defined its jurisdiction as extending over all the country north of the Humber, except the Border, which remained under the authority of the Wardens of the Marches, and the palatinate of Lancaster. In this large region it exercised the power of Star Chamber in suppressing riot and supervising administration. As a court it had not only criminal but a very extensive civil jurisdiction, so popular, indeed, that it was said at the end of the sixteenth century to handle 2,000 cases a year. The Council was popular not only with private suitors in general but the people of York in particular. For it settled permanently there, as the most convenient administrative centre, and the city thus acquired the distinction and profit of a provincial capital ⟨60⟩. The gentry of the

North thought less well of the Council: they felt the rough, administrative edge of its functions and resented the prodding interference to which it subjected them. In the main, however, the Council of the North secured the objects for which its members were sworn to strive, namely 'the quietness and good governance of the people'.

Another region which required the special remedy of a local council was Wales and the Marches. Here the Council in the Marches of Wales grew, like the Council of the North, out of the council which administered the Yorkist estates in the region and acquired a formal and continuous existence in the reign of Henry VIII. With a wide jurisdiction extending not only over Wales but the English border shires (except, after 1569, Cheshire), it performed much the same functions as the Council of the North. Because the military power of the magnates had been more effectively destroyed in Wales, and the country, after the Union, was far more peaceful than the North, this Council had rather less political significance as an instrument of royal domination. Nevertheless, the administrative and judicial business of the Council in the Marches remained important and sufficed to make Ludlow, where it chiefly sat, a provincial capital in a modest way ⟨61, 62, 63⟩.

Besides the regional councils the Tudors also created another court which, though not properly a conciliar court, formed part of the fabric of conciliar government. This was the Court of High Commission, an ecclesiastical tribunal which occupied in the church something like the place of Star Chamber in the state. It began not as a court but a body of commissioners charged by Henry VIII with the exercise of his supremacy over the church. These commissioners had, in the first place, to enforce the ecclesiastical policy of the crown; and the Commission always remained the most potent engine of ecclesiastical discipline, as the puritans discovered later on. Although at first informal the Commission gradually adopted regular sessions and uniform procedures until by 1580 it had acquired the attributes of a formal court. One reason for this development was that, like Star Chamber, it had become popular with private suitors, who valued the advantages it possessed over the ordinary church courts, particularly its speed and ability to inflict fines and imprisonment. The Court provides a further illustration of the centralising tendencies of the Tudors, of their success in obtaining a more complete obedience than any rulers before them not only to the will but the detailed policies of the central government.

Apart from developing the machinery of conciliar government the Tudors did not greatly change the administrative apparatus to which they had succeeded; and their attempts to reorganise the administration of finance were a partial failure. Throughout the period the Exchequer, with

31

its time-honoured and time-wasting routines, stood in the way of business-like accounting. Henry VIII's minister Thomas Cromwell tried to meet the difficulty by creating a number of new financial departments in the form of courts, each charged with superintending different branches of revenue. Their organisation and methods of account were modelled on those of the Duchy of Lancaster, which administered a vast nexus of royal estates.

Cromwell's system, however, did not long survive his downfall. It came under fire from conservative critics, the most formidable of whom were the officers of the Exchequer. The motive of their opposition seems to have been chiefly that of personal profit, of their pay. Before the nineteenth century governments could not afford to pay their servants sufficient wages or salaries: they rewarded them by means that seemed, misleadingly, to make less demands on the pocket, such as free board or diet at court or the right to certain perquisites, like the four fingers of wine allowed the officers of the royal buttery from every bottle opened there; or, more happily, by passing the burden elsewhere. In the days when the king's clerks had also been clerics it had been possible to reward them at the expense of the church, in the form of good livings. In the sixteenth century, however, the administration became laicised and this means no longer served. Fees now became the most important source of income for many royal officers. This had important consequences. The government's officers now had a vested interest in maintaining the paper-work of their office and preventing administrative short cuts that might cut short their profits. Moreover, many offices were regarded as the property of their holder, enjoyed frequently on a life tenure and even capable of being bought and sold; and the crown found it therefore difficult to get rid of awkward officials, except the highest, who held their places at the king's pleasure.

No doubt the objections of the old officials of the Exchequer had their effect in the reorganisation of 1554, which took the form of conservative compromise. The Exchequer was restored to its ancient central position in charge of the royal revenues and, with one exception, Cromwell's courts were merged into it. This arrangement may be called a compromise, not a victory for the Exchequer, in that new sub-departments were established within it and provided an efficient machinery for handling at least part of the revenue. Yet the Exchequer was only partly reformed: the ancient 'course' remained in being. Even the strong Tudor monarchy was not complete master of its own house.

These defects of the professional administration explain in part why the Tudors depended so much on the services of private persons. Some of the greatest administrative achievements of the age were carried through by special commissioners appointed for the purpose and drawn in many cases from the local gentry: the impressive survey of church property, known as the *Valor Ecclesiasticus*, came into being and the vast operation of dissolving the monasteries and dispersing their wealth was conducted by this means.

In local government the success of the Tudors' administration chiefly depended on their ability to enlist the voluntary and unpaid, though not necessarily unrewarded, services of the landowners. Their only real innovation was to create the office of lord lieutenant. Usually a local magnate, he was responsible for controlling the military forces of the shire and became, by virtue of his local status and royal trust, its greatest dignitary. However, what distinguished the Tudors' handling of local affairs was the central importance they attributed to the justices of the peace. The duties of this office now received such a vast extension that the justices became the virtual rulers of the countryside. Hitherto they had served, as their title suggests, mainly judicial functions in enforcing the law and keeping the peace. On top of these the Tudors, particularly Elizabeth, piled a great and variegated burden of administrative duties: the regulation of beggars, ale-houses, wages, prices, corn-dealers, apprentices, recusants, the maintenance of bridges and—heaviest of all—the organisation of poor relief ⟨66⟩.

To cope with these new responsibilities the justices had to develop a more flexible organisation. Their most formal meetings as a court took place four times a year—hence the term quarter sessions—when they sat to hear cases with a jury and full legal ceremony; and these became, next to the assizes, the most solemn occasions of the county calendar. But much of their business, though not all, could be transacted summarily and without a jury by one or two justices, acting apart from the sessions. The device of the *quorum* provided some safeguard against the abuse of power by ignorant amateurs, for in every commission of the peace the government nominated some experienced members, at least one of whom had to be present to validate any important act of authority. Only few could aspire to the *quorum*, but the office of justice, in spite of its burdens, became so sought after as the symbol of social status that the numbers on the commission rose from less than ten to forty or fifty and more, including all the gentry of any pretensions.

The employment of an amateur and unpaid local administration presented a problem of control. This was met in various ways. A judicial supervision was exercised by the central courts and judges of assize. The Privy Council and, where appropriate, the provincial councils harried the justices into performing their administrative functions. The system had great merits. It was cheap: it provided an administration remarkably well informed about local conditions and in close touch with the people it governed; and it trained the gentry to a sense of political and social responsibility. No people so steeped in public affairs could become the passive and indifferent subjects of bureaucratic despotism.

The worse side of local administration appeared lower down, below the level of shire and justices. The Tudors cut out the old enclaves of liberties and franchises, putting the parish into the centre of the picture. At this level public service was amateur, though not voluntary. The inhabitants themselves had to perform the duties of overseers of the poor, surveyors of the highways, or constables; if the parochial roads needed repair they had to provide the labour, up to six days' work a year. (See *Transport*, pp. 15–16.) Thus the last link in the administrative chain was fragile, forged by rustic Dogberries, hovering on the verges of incompetence. Yet the parish had the merit of forming a true community, possessing some elements of self-government; though in the main real control lay in the hands of the justices who virtually nominated the parish officers, except the churchwardens. For the system was essentially oligarchic. This is also true of the municipal corporations, exempted by their charters from the jurisdiction of the shire justices: here, too, the general tendency was to restrict the rights of self-government to a small body of the more substantial citizens. Whatever its defects, the system served the needs of a fairly stable and predominantly rural society: it survived in the towns until 1835; and quarter sessions continued to rule the shires until the introduction of county councils in 1888.

The fortunes of the courts of law, like those of local government, show how far the Tudors were from making themselves absolute. Although the conciliar courts, like Star Chamber, presented the appearance of a rival jurisdiction, they generally served the interests of the common law; and did so because they served the cause of law-abidingness. The development of Chancery supplemented rather than rivalled the common law and offered remedies when none could be obtained elsewhere. It protected copyhold tenures, for example, and developed a law of trusts, neither of which came within the jurisdiction of the ordinary courts. Even the competition of the conciliar courts and Chancery did the common law a service by spurring it to improve itself and learn from their practice. By the end of the Tudor period the common law had been revitalised. The Inns of Court enjoyed a golden age: a number of distinguished lawyers devoted themselves to refining and developing procedure and principles; and they prepared the way for the great work of Sir Edward Coke, who first began to publish his *Reports* in 1600 ⟨68⟩. Thus the deep medieval respect for the law survived.

Equally important was not only the survival but development of Parliament ⟨71, 72⟩, at a time when parliamentary institutions were generally declining in Europe, giving way before monarchical absolutism. For a while after the Wars of the Roses Parliaments were summoned less frequently, partly because there was no longer an aristocratic opposition to demand them, partly because the king was able to manage with his ordinary revenues from crown lands—greatly increased by recent confiscations—customs, feudal rights such as wardships, and the profits of justice. But the king still found them indispensable for certain objects: he needed their sanction for his legislative acts and, in the case of the Yorkist kings and Henry VII, for validating his title; he needed them also to authorise exceptional taxation, as in time of war. The nobility and landed gentry, too, had an interest in preserving Parliament; for, unlike their compeers in many continental countries, they had not secured exemption from direct taxation. Attempts to circumvent Parliament could provoke stubborn opposition at times when the country seemed at its most docile, as Wolsey found in 1524 when he was obliged to withdraw his proposals for levying a forced loan.

Although Parliament survived, its meetings, until 1529, remained infrequent; and, since infrequent Parliaments meant infrequent taxes, the country was content. The initiative that changed Parliament from an occasional resource to an essential partner in government came not from the country but the king. Henry VIII needed its legislative authority to secure his supremacy over the church. The importance of the Reformation Parliament, which sat—though not continuously—from 1529 to 1536, lay not merely in its unprecedented length but in the acts of sovereign power in which it participated. By modern standards, meetings were still rare and sessions short: in the forty-five years of Elizabeth's reign it actually sat 140 weeks; but, in proportion to the length of reign, this is three times as long as the Parliaments of Henry VII.

Meanwhile, Parliament was developing its procedure, privileges and form. The House of Lords took its modern shape in the reign of Henry VIII, as councillors and ministers ceased to attend, unless they were themselves peers, and the dissolution of the monasteries left the spiritual lords in a minority. At the same time the House of Commons became the real forum of political debate. A number of privy councillors were now always maintained in the House to guide its discussions. The importance of the Commons' business led them to develop a consistent procedure for its dispatch. The practice of reading bills three times became normal early in Elizabeth's reign, voting by division took the place of acclamation, and the rules of debate were elaborated.

The Commons also acquired well-defined privileges. Although in form they were a gift from the crown that could be withdrawn, they were in practice well established by the end of the sixteenth century and such disputes as they aroused concerned their limits rather than substance. Through the Speaker, who provided the regular means of communication between government and Commons, members enjoyed freedom of access to the sovereign. Because attendance at Parliament took precedence over all other obligations members also enjoyed freedom from arrest. The House exercised the right to discipline its own members by way of fine or even expulsion or imprisonment; and, more controversially, extended its power over non-members accused of showing contempt for its privileges. The House also acquired the right to decide disputed elections and the fitness of members to sit: a right contested by the crown and not fully established until 1604.

The most important of parliamentary privileges was also the most difficult to define. This was freedom of speech, without which Parliament would be no more than a ratifying assembly. The first formal request for the privilege is not recorded until 1523; but by the beginning of Elizabeth's reign the right was established. However, the Queen, taking her stand on traditional practice, maintained that the right had limits. Members should be free to speak as they wished on matters that were a proper subject of discussion; but matters touching the royal prerogative, such as foreign policy, ecclesiastical affairs, or the succession, should be raised only with royal consent. The scope of this privilege clearly raised a fundamental constitutional issue. For the time being Elizabeth succeeded in imposing her interpretation.

The importance of the Commons was further reflected by the striking expansion in their numbers, which increased by more than half during the sixteenth century to make a total of 462. The interest, however, of this increase lies less in the number than in the character of the new members. By far the greatest part of the new members were elected by boroughs newly enfranchised by the crown, exercising its undoubted right. Yet for the most part these new members were not burgesses, in the social sense of the term, but country gentlemen. The gentry could never satisfy their aspirations from the county seats alone, which numbered less than a hundred: hence from early in the fifteenth century they had begun to move into the borough seats; and when there were not enough of these within easy reach they pressed the crown to create more. Thus many of the new members were returned by comparatively insignificant towns, elevated to the dignity of parliamentary borough not out of respect for their commerce but in order to satisfy the borough-hunger of the country gentry ⟨65⟩. This process did as much as the development of procedure and privileges to make the Commons an effective and formidable body. The House was now less blinkered by local interests; and, being composed not of insignificant townsmen but predominantly of gentlemen of some standing, nurtured in the common law and experienced in local affairs, it was not likely to be a compliant instrument of royal power.

The efforts made by the Tudors to influence and manage the Commons were a tribute to its independence as well as importance. On the whole they did not try systematically to influence elections but were more concerned to secure the return of a small body of councillors and other royal servants who could provide a nucleus of government supporters to guide and influence the House. They also found it important to obtain a favourable Speaker, who indeed at this period regarded himself as a servant of the crown as well as the House. Such management did not produce servile Parliaments: taxes were rarely granted easily, and even the formidable Henry VIII met obstinate opposition on occasion. Opposition became more frequent and serious under his successors, when the nation was more divided, particularly by issues of religion and foreign affairs. Mary found herself checked in her hopes of restoring the monastic endowments: Elizabeth had to accept, at the beginning of her reign, a more Protestant religious settlement than she had contemplated and, at the end, had to surrender completely to the Commons' protests about monopolies. Yet one should not dwell on the disputes and neglect the harmony between Elizabeth and her Parliaments. The consistent critics were few and mostly thwarted: they had their say and the Queen, for the most part, had her way.

Tudor government displayed a centaur-like mixture of absolutism and constitutionalism, order and liberty: on the one part the formidable revival of royal power, the process of centralisation and national consolidation at the expense of medieval fractionalism; on the other the revival of the common law, the vital development of Parliament, the reinvigoration of local institutions. Its character was best described by Sir Thomas Smith who, writing in Elizabeth's reign, called it a mixed form of government in which supreme power rested in the partnership of King-in-Parliament. England could now be described as a national, sovereign state, church and barons had been brought under control, the country united. These great changes had been carried through, however, not by overturning but by revitalising the old institutions and evolving from them a government fit for new conditions. The revolution in the state had been achieved without a revolution in government.

*　　*　　*

When revolution came, in the seventeenth century, it took another form, directed not towards but against monarchical absolutism. Even so it was a preserving, not, in the long run, a radical revolution. It had its radical moments—civil war, a king executed, another exiled, a republic, even a written constitution—but in the end they were mostly repudiated and historical continuity maintained. The revolutionary years produced little in the way of new institutions: they destroyed some; but their main consequence lay in changing the relationships between existing institutions, particularly between king, Parliament and courts, and between central and local authorities. The tradition of harmony eventually prevailed, though in a different form, that of constitutional monarchy, in which Parliament had become an equal and, on ultimate issues, the dominant partner.

Harmony, however, was only re-established after years of discord in which it appeared at times as if the old partnership would be completely destroyed. At first the ambiguities of Tudor government seemed likely to be resolved in favour of Stuart absolutism. For, already becoming precarious under Elizabeth, the system could not stand the strain imposed by her less trusted and less competent successors, a more restless and aspiring Commons, and deeply disputed policies ⟨73, 75⟩. By 1629 king and Commons were set so completely at odds that Charles I tried to resolve the conflict by dispensing with Parliament; and under the impulse of two administrative martinets, William Laud, who became Archbishop of Canterbury in 1633, and Sir Thomas Wentworth, later Earl of Strafford, church and state were subjected to a bracing regimen exercised through the conciliar courts ⟨76, 77⟩. For all its administrative merits this 'Eleven Years' Tyranny' aroused in the long run an overwhelming opposition because it threatened the traditional liberties of the possessing classes. Its weaknesses were exposed when, in 1639, a Scottish war forced the king to appeal to the country: he met a stubborn refusal to co-operate and a universal demand for a Parliament. Defeated by the Scots, Charles I had to capitulate at home. In November 1640 the Long Parliament met and the English Revolution began.

In ten decisive months the country changed course from absolutism to constitutionalism. The arbitrary practices of Charles I were declared illegal, his claim to an overriding sovereignty denied, and his rights brought within the law. The Long Parliament believed it was restoring the idealised Tudor partnership; but in spite of this conservative aim it went on to a work of destruction which made partnership under the old terms impossible. For experience had shown that it was not enough to state the law: as long as the king possessed the conciliar courts he could defy it. And so, in spite of its virtues, the whole machinery of conciliar government, through which England had been ruled for a century and a half, was swept away. Its destruction left a balance of power between king, Parliament and common-law courts. The king could no longer, it was hoped, override statute, tax without consent, or imprison without trial; Parliament could not be dispensed with, but made no claim to exercise executive power or impose ministers on the king; the courts stood somewhat in the position of arbiter; and the liberties of the subject were protected from the arbitrary encroachment of a sovereign power.

By August 1641 the Long Parliament had established the basis on which England was to be governed for nearly two centuries to come; but nearly fifty years of civil war, revolution and discord had to pass before it was firmly secured. Those years were more than a hiatus in the evolution of English government: they provided the experience without which the settlement of 1688 could not have succeeded. They taught the propertied classes the value of a balanced power and the danger of upsetting it. For when one party in the Long Parliament, distrusting the intentions of Charles I, went on to claim for Parliament the sovereignty it had denied the king, they destroyed the original unity of the Commons and forced those who feared party tyranny as much as royal tyranny to rally to the crown. In 1642 their conflict led to civil war.

The Civil War reinforced the lesson; for neither of the original contestants won. Victory went to the army which the Parliamentarians raised but which, interpreting the struggle in apocalyptic terms as a people's crusade to build a new Jerusalem, had been disillusioned with the narrow, traditional liberties cherished by their employers. Having won the war, they turned their arms on Parliament, executed the king in 1649 as an enemy of the people—and, as they thought, of God ⟨81⟩—abolished both monarchy and House of Lords, and established, they hoped, the reign of political and religious liberty ⟨84⟩.

Nobility and gentry found the aims of the army disagreeable and their practice worse. The soldiers could only maintain power by force and, by a cruel paradox, had to uphold liberty by a military dictatorship. Although their general, Oliver Cromwell, tried to reconcile army and country by adopting a written constitution that restored some of the traditional forms of government he had to rely ultimately on the sword and undertake acts as arbitrary as any attempted by Charles I ⟨86, 87⟩.

Thus, when Cromwell's death and disputes in the army allowed the Royalists and Parliamentarians to reassert themselves ⟨88, 89⟩, they had learned to return to the common basis established in 1641 and work out their disputes within its limits. The Restoration of 1660 restored the constitution more or less as it had stood at the end of the Long Parliament's first session, before division had set in. In principle it did not represent the triumph of any one party; and in its moderation and ability to reconcile conflicting views the settlement set the standard which English politics were henceforth to follow. The English Revolution, unlike the French, did not divide the country into two irreconcilable nations which no regime could unite.

In practice, however, the Restoration reacted too strongly against the radicalism of the Interregnum. A wave of royalist enthusiasm prevented conditions being imposed on the restored Stuarts; and in the next thirty years the conflict of parties enabled them to threaten the country with a new royal absolutism. When James II used the vaguely defined dispensing and suspending powers to subvert the established church, the danger was brought home ⟨94⟩. In 1688, as in 1640, the king was faced by a universal opposition. It led to the flight of James, the accession of William and Mary, and a new constitutional settlement.

This Glorious Revolution merits its name because it at last concluded the stormy age of constitutional conflict and inaugurated an Augustan peace. The whole tone of the settlement that followed it was profoundly conservative, faithful to the central constitutional developments of the preceding half-century and, above all, designed to attract the widest range of loyalties. It attempted no doctrinaire pronouncements. Indeed the Bill of Rights ⟨95⟩, which was the foundation charter of the regime, seems English to the point of caricature in its sense of compromise, its empiricism, reluctance to generalise, even taciturnity. It recognised that James was no longer king and offered the crown to William and Mary; and apart from this, despite its name, did not embark on any general statement about rights, but recited a list of the ways in which James had acted illegally. In fact, far from breaking new ground, the makers of the settlement tried to disguise the fact that a revolution had occurred at all.

In great measure this interpretation was correct. Much of the legislation now adopted merely made explicit what had hitherto been implicit or plugged holes in the constitutional defences that had not been observed until the Stuarts exploited them. This is clearly true in the condemnation of the suspending and dispensing powers. It is true, also, in the practice adopted in 1689 and made statutory in 1701 whereby the judges could no longer be dismissed at the king's pleasure; for clearly the law could not be safe without an independent judiciary.

On the other hand the legislation of this period also did more than just underline the settlement of 1660. It weighted the constitutional balance further against the king. Take the control of the armed forces, one of the most crucial issues in government. Now it was declared that the maintenance of a standing army in time of peace without consent of Parliament was against the law; and the Mutiny Act of 1689 provided a further safeguard by making parliamentary sanction necessary to give legal authority to any code of military discipline. Henceforward the armed forces were no longer the king's almost private concern, but the property of

40

the nation and within the pale of the civil constitution. How important this provision was may be appreciated by comparison with the history of Prussia, where no such rules applied.

Moreover, the circumstances of the Revolution deprived the monarchy of some of its mystical prestige. It was clear that William and Mary owed their title primarily to Parliament; and this dependence became still more clear later in the case of the Hanoverians. The principle of Protestant Succession, made statutory by the Act of Settlement of 1701, had itself implications which lowered the status of monarchy, for it dictated the monarch's religion. This implied that he was no longer master but servant of the nation and had to wear its livery. The revised Coronation Oath, by which the king now swore to rule 'according to the statutes in Parliament agreed on', made the point that he was below, not above, the law.

Yet the Revolution did not leave the king a figurehead. He had, admittedly, lost his power to set aside the law; the independence of Parliament had been vindicated and his ability to influence it limited by a new Triennial Act which prevented his extending the life of Parliament beyond three years. Faced with the unprecedented burden of the French wars, William III had to summon Parliament annually and allow it to an increasing extent to determine how he should spend the revenues it voted or the loans it authorised. By 1697 his financial discretion was practically limited to the revenues voted in the form of the Civil List for the upkeep of the civil administration and royal household. But, with all this, government remained the king's business. He was still head of the executive, responsible for making policy and carrying it out. In theory and to a great extent in fact he chose his own ministers. If his choice was limited by the need to find men who could command a following in Parliament, Parliament could not force on him, certainly for any length of time, a minister whom he did not want. While the Revolution finally secured the independence of Parliament and the judges, it did not deprive the king of his independence.

*   *   *

Circumstances favoured this settlement. Between the end of the War of Spanish Succession and the American Revolution few critical issues arose to excite deep political passions. Religious passions, too, so powerful earlier, abated after the Revolution. But in this respect policy as well as chance made a contribution. One reason for the disharmony that had followed the Restoration lay in the attempt to suppress protestant nonconformists by penal laws that prohibited their public worship and subjected them to civil disabilities. After the Revolution a partial remedy was offered by the Toleration Act which gave them almost unrestricted freedom of worship. Their politics, however, were still suspect and they did not therefore yet receive equal civil rights: they were barred from the English universities and municipal office. Yet, except for a short harassing period in Queen Anne's reign, even these penal laws were not rigorously applied and after 1727 it became the practice to pass Indemnity Acts which enabled dissenters to hold public office without fear of prosecution. The problem of nonconformity thus ceased to disturb politics; and public life was the healthier for it.

Yet the cooling of political and religious passions does not fully explain the harmony of the Augustan Age that followed the Revolution. Part of the answer must also lie in the greater confidence that could now be felt in the crown since its powers of doing harm had been diminished. There still existed areas of dispute, because it was easier to define what the king could not do than what he could. But the country now had the security that the king must be a Protestant; and both precedent and law made it virtually impossible that he should make any serious attempt to subvert the constitution.

Even so, co-operation between king and Parliament could not be achieved without effort. Unless it was organised and managed Parliament would be composed of an incoherent mass of members and incapable of giving consistent support to any policy. The Tudors had seen this; so had the opponents of the Stuarts. After the Restoration, when Parliament had clearly become the centre of public business, both ministers and their rivals attempted to build up an organised following of members on whose consistent support they hoped to rely. In the fierce conflicts of Charles II's reign such a following came to be enlisted by inviting members to rally round a common programme or set of principles, in other words by forming a party. The classic Whig and Tory parties now emerged. But after the Revolution and still more after the Hanoverian succession the appeal to party feeling provided a fragile means of securing support. Party implied an attitude of mind rather than an organisation: it required an extreme crisis and unusual leadership to create even the most elementary forms of organisation; and with the general avoidance of fundamental issues that characterised the eighteenth century the ties of party grew slack and party labels provided no reliable guide to the actual allegiance of the members who bore them. In these conditions the modern method of appointing ministers from a party which commands a majority in Parliament was quite inapplicable: indeed, in that stark form, it was quite unthinkable, for ministers still regarded themselves as servants of the king, not of party.

The needs of government were harmonised with the will of Parliament by other means, particularly the system of 'influence'. Since ministers could not create a reliable following of members by appealing to principle they had to do it by exploiting all the honours and rewards that it was in the king's power to give. Even the House of Lords was susceptible to an appeal of this sort. The greatest nobleman might still covet the distinctions that only the king could confer, and might desire rewards for the innumerable dependants and clients attached to any great man. Bishoprics, too, were at least in part the reward of political loyalty; the bishops were regarded as servants of the crown and depended on to provide, through thick and thin, solid votes for the administration. To members of the House of Commons the ministry could offer pensions, places or offices that were in the king's patronage, or titles and other dignities as the reward of loyalty. Patronage, first deployed systematically in the reign of Charles II, became so important an element in the craft of parliamentary management that, under the Hanoverians, its judicious distribution was one of the chief functions of the First Lord of the Treasury—one reason why he tended to become the most important minister. The governments of the eighteenth century were fortunate that the administrative service had expanded, and therefore constituted a capacious reservoir of *pourboires* to which they controlled the taps. Members of the Commons could hope for pensions or places or contracts for themselves or their dependants in return for their votes. Civil servants sitting in the House were indeed expected to support the government, and all ministries tried to maintain there a substantial body of placemen, some hundred or two hundred members whose votes could be depended on.

The operation of influence also reached down to the electorate. It was not enough to manage the members once elected: it was necessary for the administration to secure the election of the right sort of members, pledged to support it. The great variety of electoral rights and types of constituencies made this a complex task, which required great expertise. A general distinction may be drawn between the counties and boroughs. The franchise in the counties, fixed in the fifteenth century (see p. 13), preserved them from the grosser forms of corruption and the direct influence of the crown, so that the county members were always regarded as the most independent part of the Commons. This is not to say that the county voters were not subjected to influence, but it was a subtle influence by which social inferiors deferred to the wishes intimated to them by their betters in the local hierarchy; and indeed they were rarely called on to exercise their franchise because the dominating families or interests usually tried to avoid contests.

In the boroughs there was none of this uniformity, for no general qualifications for the franchise had ever been laid down by law (cf. *The Town*, p. 57). Some boroughs might have a large electorate: in some it

43

might be a mere handful; in others the choice of members might be vested solely in the mayor and corporation ⟨115, 116⟩. The ways of influencing a borough were infinite. A corporation could be swayed by an appeal to its interests, in the way, perhaps, of advantages for its trade. Voters in general might be under strong compulsion to vote for a government candidate if some branch of the administration, such as the admiralty, happened to be the largest employer in the borough and an adverse vote—there being no secrecy—was likely to cost them their livelihood. If the electorate was small, individual votes had to be bought, not by money necessarily, but by favours or offices—in this respect the more humble places in the revenue departments provided useful tender of a small denomination ⟨123⟩.

In spite of its resources the administration by no means had all its own way in the boroughs. The treasury or admiralty could only be sure of controlling a handful of them on its own. In order to secure the election of loyal supporters the government had to enlist the goodwill of the many private persons, who either had boroughs completely in their pockets or exercised a strong influence over them ⟨117⟩. This was an important factor. Because the government did not have anything like a monopoly of influence, it could not use it to establish a despotism by the back door. Admittedly ministries always won their general elections, but that was only because every election was preceded by protracted negotiations and bargains with the private patrons of boroughs: in other words no ministry could maintain itself if it disregarded the dominant interests in the country.

This helps to explain the importance of the House of Lords in the eighteenth century. During the previous century it had been eclipsed by the advance of the Commons and at times reduced to a secondary role, but, for a number of reasons, had since recovered. One reason for this lies in the extensive political influence that the Lords possessed in the constituencies, with the result that, though the House, as such, was inferior in power to the Commons, it had in practice a considerable control over the lower House extending well beyond its legal powers. It was therefore important for any ministry to retain the goodwill of the Lords; and not only as a means of influencing the Commons, but as a means of blocking in a polite way measures which it might be tactless to oppose lower down. And most ministers sat in the Lords, not in the Commons.

The power of influence should not be exaggerated. It contributed to the harmony that government required; and yet did not reduce Parliament to a state of dependence. If questions of principle were allowed to arise the chains of influence proved weak to constrain the members. Hence the concern of governments to avoid controversial issues; hence, too, the slender legislative output of Hanoverian Parliaments.

This explains also the great respect that governments showed for local autonomy. The revolution of the seventeenth century had been inspired to a great extent by resentment of central control, and with the destruction of the conciliar system the gentry had liberated themselves from the tutelage of Whitehall. Since then no government that wanted to remain at peace with the Commons interfered with the conduct of local government except by tactful means. Not that there was no control or co-ordination. The judges of assize continued to exercise their general supervision and ministers still issued instructions to the justices, as at the time of the rebellion of the Forty-five; but the real control was indirect, through the close relationship existing between the members of the Commons and the local justices. Even so, in the eighteenth century local government enjoyed a greater autonomy and freedom of development than at any other time. The independence enjoyed by quarter sessions, municipal corporations and other privileged bodies like the universities, provided yet another element in the constitutional balance through which English liberties were thought to be secured.

This system of government made possible the security and enlargement of civil liberties. In the first place it afforded the essentials, the independence of the courts and the rule of law. The independence of the judges in turn made possible the effective protection of personal liberty, even without the help of the legislature. Already the old procedure of *habeas corpus* had been made more effective by an Act of 1679 and the Bill of Rights: and it was actively applied by the courts. In Somersett's case of 1772 the procedure not only secured the liberation of a negro slave who was being detained by his master on a ship in the Thames but the famous and authoritative opinion of the court that the very institution of slavery was contrary to the law of England. In the cases that arose from the attempts of the government to suppress the attacks made on it by John Wilkes the courts showed equal readiness to defend individual liberty against the executive, by finding that powers of arrest and of seizing papers customarily employed by the Secretaries of State had no basis in law ⟨109⟩.

The more specifically political liberties were not so well established. The destruction of the conciliar courts had not, for example, been followed immediately by freedom of the press. Censorship had been re-established by parliamentary authority in the form of Licensing Acts, which had been renewed after the Revolution. When at last the Commons in 1695 refused to renew the Licensing Act they did so less because they disapproved of censorship in principle than because of the irritation, exactions and petty annoyances that were caused in its enforcement. Even then, although the press enjoyed a freedom rare in Europe, it was still limited by the conservative traditions of the common law. Writers were subject to the law of libel, and in the view of the judges any criticism of the government

45

could be construed as a libel. The courts could enforce this interpretation because under the old law of libel it was the function of the judge, not the jury, to decide whether any particular publication was libellous. By this means the press remained subject to penalties long after public opinion had ceased to be scandalised by open criticism of the government. The law was not brought into harmony with public opinion until 1792, when Fox's Libel Act transferred the right of determining libel from judge to jury and thus, because the public was more liberal than the courts, effectively established the liberty of the press.

One of the necessary political liberties, the right of public meeting, was established only in the nineteenth century. Although public meetings were held, particularly in connexion with preparing petitions to Parliament, and although the law did not forbid them, they were given no special protection.

Eighteenth-century government had many disreputable features: it was narrow, exclusive, offering privileges to birth, rank and, to some extent, wealth; and harsh, sometimes barbaric, justice to the poor. Yet, though its values differed from those of later generations, its better habits survived. Above all it formulated and transmitted a mode of conducting politics which has become part of the English tradition: it taught Englishmen the language of parliamentary politics, the habit of treating government as a subject of reasoned discussion, and political life as a matter—to use Aristotle's phrase—'of ruling and being ruled in turn'. It proved to the country and to Europe that absolutism was not the only viable form of government even for a great power. It taught the country confidence in its institutions and it firmly entrenched the precedents which later broadened out into parliamentary democracy.

*   *   *

Another achievement of this period was to establish at last a harmonious relationship between England and Scotland. Since the sixteenth century the two had been drawn more closely together. The Reformation broke the old Franco-Scottish alliance, for the Protestants could impose their will only with the help of their fellows in England ⟨64⟩; and, after 1560, the long hostility came to an end. In 1603 this new understanding was sealed by the accession of James VI to the English throne. In the following years the development of English overseas trade and colonies led Scottish merchants to appreciate the benefits they might secure from economic integration.

These new conditions took long to promote the union they made possible. Although protestantism created a common bond, the different forms

46

which it took in each country created a new tension. The Scottish Reformation, more extreme than the English, had led to a Presbyterian church in which the traditional authority of the bishops was replaced by that of a representative General Assembly. This system could not easily endure side by side with the episcopal organisation of the Anglican church: each tried at some stage to impose itself on the other. Charles I introduced some conformity between them; and provoked the Scottish revolution and National Covenant of 1638. The Covenanters tried to secure themselves by supporting a presbyterian regime in England and provoked the Cromwellian occupation, which destroyed their power and delivered them helpless again in 1660 to the Stuarts.

Even the union of the crowns did not prove a universal blessing, particularly to the Scots. It gave them greater security, because the king, safe in London, enjoying the resources of a great monarchy, could at last impose order on his nobility; and common rights of citizenship provided some advantage. On the other hand Scotland was now governed by remote control from London, and the Stuarts, consolidating their hold in Parliament through the Lords of the Articles, established an effective absolutism which lasted—except for the Covenanting interlude—until 1689.

Economic interests also caused disputes. The English Parliament refused to grant more than the union of crowns and resolutely barred the Scots from the benefits of English colonial trade. After the Restoration English policy became even more exclusive and although Glasgow developed a substantial trade with America it remained illegal and hazardous.

The Revolution of 1688 eased some of these tensions but created new. It enabled the General Assembly to abolish episcopacy, reintroduced by the Stuarts, and restore the Presbyterian church to its independence; and the Scottish Parliament—reinforced since 1587 by representatives of the shires—to abolish the Committee of the Articles and secure independence from Whitehall. But this independence made it difficult for the government in London to override Scottish interests. When the French war damaged Scottish trade and the failure of the ambitious 'Darien' company—intended to rival the East India Company—was attributed to English spite, the Parliament of 1703 determined to demonstrate the value of the Scottish connexion. It threatened that, unless her interests were respected, Scotland would adopt a separate foreign policy and a different ruling house.

This threat made it clear that under constitutional monarchy the union of crowns alone did not suffice; and thus, because neither country could afford a separation, the crisis started negotiations for a closer union. In 1707 a bargain was struck; and the Act of Union established the basis on which the relationship of England and Scotland still stands ⟨97⟩.

GOVERNMENT

Each country gained something. England gained the political unity of the island, for the Scots accepted the Hanoverian succession, relinquished their Parliament, and now sent representatives to the newly-styled Parliament of Great Britain at Westminster. The dominant ecclesiastical and economic interests of Scotland also profited: the Presbyterians won the guarantee that the maintenance of their established church would be treated as a fundamental condition of the Union; and the Scottish merchants received commercial equality with the English. Scots in general were appeased by the guarantee that their law would be respected and legal institutions preserved.

This act of statesmanship redeemed the mistakes of the past. Although not at first popular nor immediately followed by the expected prosperity, the Union survived the early years of strain because it respected the essential institutions to which Scottish patriotism attached itself—the Scottish Parliament had not enjoyed a real independence long enough to entrench itself in the native tradition. And so the Jacobite risings of 1715 and 1745, though alarming, did not receive wide support in Scotland.

The English were thought guilty of sharp practice when, in spite of the terms of the Union, the House of Lords took cognisance of appeals from Scotland. But otherwise the Scottish legal system was respected and the great advances made since the sixteenth century maintained. Justice remained centralised in Edinburgh. This had been achieved in civil affairs in 1532 when James V created the Court of Session, staffed with professional judges; and, reorganised in the nineteenth century, this court, presided over by the Lord President and Lord Justice Clerk, remains the supreme civil court of Scotland. The criminal jurisdiction of the Justiciar or Lord Justice-General had been given a permanent establishment in Edinburgh in 1524; and this arrangement was preserved when in 1671 his powers were vested in the High Court of Justiciary—still the supreme criminal court of Scotland. Nor were the lower courts assimilated to the English model. The sheriffs' courts remained the most important, exercising—as they do still—a civil and criminal jurisdiction quite unparalleled by any inferior court in England: by contrast, the justices of the peace, introduced by James VI, remained of minor importance.

The survival of the courts secured also the survival of the Scottish law. This had, since the sixteenth century and under the influence of French and Dutch law, undergone an extensive reconstruction, particularly at the hands of Viscount Stair, and emerged an enlightened instrument, capable of holding its own in the modern world. Although the accumulation of statute law has since brought the practice of the two countries closer, Scottish law still displays marked differences of procedure and substance.

48

After the middle of the eighteenth century Scotland entered on a golden age of intellectual and economic activity. When the Jacobite risings had been suppressed the Highlands ceased to threaten the advance of civilisation. The building of roads, the Disarming Act which forbade the wearing of Highland dress and prohibited Highland customs, the progress of the economy, broke down the authority of the clans and turned the militant tribesmen into peaceful tenants: their savagery dissolved in a romantic twilight.

In the last hundred years the harmonious relations that the English enjoyed with both Scotland and Wales have been strained by the development of Scottish and Welsh nationalism. In both countries political reform provided the opportunity for self-expression, and a cultural revival stimulated a passionate concern for native tradition and achievement. In these conditions the expansion of the central administration—so marked since the early nineteenth century—provoked a reaction against the increasing dependence on Whitehall and a demand for a greater local autonomy. In its extreme form this nationalism has bred political parties devoted to a programme of Home Rule which would turn Britain into a federal state ⟨182, 183, 185⟩.

Nationalist criticism has been partly met by administrative devolution. In 1885 a regular Secretary—later Secretary of State—was appointed for Scotland; his office became the Scottish office and in 1935 was transferred to Edinburgh. For Wales—where, since 1888, bilingual teaching has been provided in the state schools—a separate Department of Education has been established and a Minister for Welsh Affairs (usually the Home Secretary) appointed, with a Minister of State to assist him. The demand for separate Parliaments for domestic affairs has met with less response: at the most the Scottish and Welsh Standing Committees at Westminster, composed of the Scottish and Welsh members, have enjoyed since 1948 more extensive powers over legislation concerning their countries, making them Parliaments within Parliament.

Parliamentary Democracy

FTER THE END OF THE EIGHTEENTH CENTURY THE AGE OF
stability, which had lasted since the Glorious Revolution, gave place to
an age of movement, in which government had to adapt itself to the demands
of a rapidly growing and rapidly changing society. The balanced, mixed
government of the Hanoverians was well adapted to the needs of a predominantly rural, stable society in which habits of deference supported the
privileges of birth and a small population made few demands on the
administrative machine. Under the pressure of an expanding urban civilisation, which lacked the old respect for rank and landed wealth, and created
new problems of administration, the system was transformed. The balance
of powers was replaced by the sovereignty of the people: in place of local
autonomy came a return to centralisation; with the immense expansion in
the range of the government's activity the handful of clerks with which its
business had formerly been transacted swelled into a great civil service.
Yet this adjustment to the needs of an urban, industrial and mobile
society was accomplished without revolution and within constitutional
limits. Although Hanoverian commentators, like the lawyer Blackstone,
regarded the constitution as changeless, almost as if it possessed
the character of a written document, in fact its greatest merit was
now shown to be its flexibility in absorbing change while preserving
tradition.

At the end of the eighteenth century, in a population of nearly ten
million, the parliamentary electorate numbered some 400,000: today it
numbers over thirty million. Revolutionary though this expansion might
seem, the constitution absorbed the shock; for the change occurred in
stages. The Reform Act of 1832 ⟨129⟩ was a modest first step, which increased the electorate by half. Moreover this increase was mostly confined to the boroughs, where the Act enfranchised the owners of property
worth £10 or more a year; and in the counties the old regime was hardly
changed. Although the new urban wealth received some representation
the landed interest retained its ancient predominance. The redistribution
of seats still left the South, which was mainly agricultural, more fully

50

represented than London and the North, where the main centres of population and industry lay. The Act, therefore, did not produce any marked change in the social composition of the Commons ⟨131⟩ nor in electoral habits: because voting was not secret and the electorate in many places still small, the methods of influence and bribery often survived ⟨132, 133⟩. Because, however, the larger electorate was more difficult to control and there were fewer seats left completely in the hands of their patrons, the Act made the House of Commons more independent of the administration.

Yet even if the first Reform Act did not immediately change the personnel or mechanism of politics it administered a shock to the old concept of mixed, balanced government; for it was carried through by the Commons, supported by the electorate ⟨130⟩, against the other partners of the balance. Once it had been shown that the constitution might be revised at the will of the electorate there could be no finality.

Nevertheless it took the greater part of a hundred years to reach full democracy. In 1867 the introduction of household franchise to the towns gave the vote to the urban artisan; but this was not extended to the counties until 1885 and manhood suffrage not established until 1918. Women first received the vote in 1918 ⟨144⟩, but only achieved electoral equality with men in 1928 ⟨145⟩. The franchise was now so wide that in 1948 the Labour government could find little more to do than abolish conditions of residence and certain rights of plural voting.

In the same period the character of parliamentary constituencies changed. Numbers, not interests and communities, now provided the basis of representation and made it necessary to reorganise the constituencies so as to achieve an equal number of voters in each. The Redistribution Act of 1867 took the first step by breaking up many of the traditional two-member constituencies and replacing them by single-member constituencies of almost equal size. In 1948 single-member constituencies were made universal, the boundaries so drawn as to give each an electorate of about 57,000, and a permanent commission established to make a periodic review in the interests of equality.

The democratic franchise was bound to change the social composition of the Commons, but it did so more slowly and less drastically than many had expected. Although property qualifications for members of the Commons were abolished in 1858 and members began to be paid in 1911, the electorate continued to favour candidates of some wealth, standing and education. The Labour Party only became a great national party after 1918. Manual workers still form a small proportion of the members of Parliament: they do not even predominate in the Labour Party, which was careful from the first not to restrict itself to working-class representatives. Thus changes in the social character of parliamentary membership have been gradual, not accompanied by a violent shock to the traditions of the House, and compatible with the continued predominance of 'respectable' interests.

*   *   *

The vast increase in the electorate, accompanied by safeguards like the Ballot Act of 1872, which abolished the ancient practice of open voting ⟨136, 137⟩, and like the various measures against bribery, put an end to the old methods of organising the electorate by means of influence. The place that influence had occupied in the past began to be taken by party. Although the history of the two traditional parties of Whigs and Tories goes back at least to the reign of Charles II, organised party arose only with the new electorate. Party differences, which had been of little importance during much of the eighteenth century, had revived later in the reign of George III, particularly in response to the French Revolution: during that time the terms Whig and Tory had acquired a renewed significance. But with the small electorate little formal organisation was yet required. Country houses provided local headquarters, family connexion recruited the members, and the House of Commons formed the club. The first Reform Act stimulated in a small way the organisation of parties in constituencies, for it provided that electors had now to be officially registered. This provision forced local politicians to pay constant attention to the electoral register; and in order to do this they had to create local organisations. The registration societies that now sprang up, particularly in the larger towns, were the first electoral organisations that were intended to have a continuous existence and not confined only to the purpose of a particular election. In towns like Leicester, where political excitement remained intense, a registration society might strike deep roots, with branches established in every ward of the town. Even so, this was only a modest development: local societies were not closely linked with a central body, except in an informal way with institutions like the Carlton Club, founded in 1831, and the Reform Club, founded in 1838.

At the same time party alignment became more important in the House of Commons after 1832. It became rarer for a member not to declare his attachment, and it soon became the practice for newspapers, in reporting debates, to assume that each member had a party label, and to publish party lists. Members met to discuss the policy of their party. These party ties, admittedly, remained weak. Between the first and second Reform Acts the private member, or back-bencher, emancipated from the influence of the crown, was not yet subjected to the yoke of party discipline. Elections were not necessarily fought on national issues, nor on party programmes, nor to support a party leader: many elections were not even

52

contested, many members were not dependent for their election on party organisation. This meant that a member had little difficulty in transferring his allegiance. Furthermore, in the middle years of the nineteenth century the development of party was set back when the Conservative Party that Peel had built up fell apart over the issue of free trade.

Party organisation on a national scale really developed after 1867. The new electorate had to be wooed by new methods, in particular by the appeal of a party programme and a party leader; and the greater frequency of electoral contests required a tighter national and local organisation. The new model was provided by the National Liberal Federation founded in 1877. This Federation was a nationally organised party with a constitution, with constituency associations affiliated to the central body, and with a programme put before and approved by an annual conference. This was the example followed later by the Labour Party, and, to a less extent, by the Conservatives.

After the second Reform Act all local contests in a general election increasingly tended to become part of a single national campaign; and this enhanced the status of the party leaders. As early as 1834, admittedly, Peel's Tamworth Manifesto received a national circulation, but this still preserved at least the fiction of being addressed only to the constituents of Tamworth; and Peel did not stump the country in support of his party's cause. Even after 1867 Disraeli remained appropriately conservative in refusing to conduct a national campaign or speak outside his own constituency. The first politician to play the role of a modern party leader was Gladstone, who in his Midlothian campaign of 1879 ⟨140⟩ shocked many people not only by the vigour of his eloquence but by his systematic and tireless tour of public speaking: he set a precedent which could not be resisted.

The development of party brought an end to the golden age which the private members enjoyed since 1832 and strengthened the authority of the Cabinet over the House of Commons. The Cabinet already had a long though obscure history behind it. Its history is difficult to trace because the Cabinet arose outside the law, not created by statute but by convention or tacit understanding. It had its probable origin early in the seventeenth century as a special committee of the Privy Council, an inner ring of the king's most confidential advisers. Although still variable in composition—as it remains—it had by the eighteenth century acquired a certain form in that it generally consisted of the heads of the most important departments, numbering, at the end of the century, about twelve; and it was these members of the Cabinet who controlled the ministry. By this time the Privy Council had lost all real executive power. However, the Cabinet had not yet acquired all the features that now characterise it. Its members regarded themselves as the king's servants, not as the servants of Parliament: they did not feel bound to resign unless they forfeited his confidence, nor to remain loyal to one another. It only became gradually the accepted view that the Cabinet ought as a rule to be unanimous and represent a single party: that its members should be responsible collectively to Parliament, not to the monarch, and resign together if unable to command a majority in the Commons; and that the sovereign should accept the Cabinet's decisions.

Another characteristic that the Cabinet gradually acquired was that it should recognise the authority of a common head or Prime Minister. Like the Cabinet the position of Prime Minister was not created by law, and like the Cabinet, it was at first unpopular and regarded even as unconstitutional. It was not until the long ministry of the younger Pitt at the end of the eighteenth century that the title at last became respectable and the position was regarded as a necessary part of the political system. From that time the Prime Minister steadily freed himself from the need to defer to the monarch's wishes and so increased his mastery over his colleagues, since it fell to him, and no longer the king, to appoint and change the ministers. The Prime Minister's power over the Cabinet was reinforced as the electorate grew larger, as parties organised themselves on a national scale, and as popular means of communication, like the cheap press, allowed party leaders to project themselves to a wide public. Even before the second Reform Act a party leader like Palmerston had been able to win an election for his followers to a great extent by the force of his national popularity. After 1867 general elections tended to become in part a vote of confidence in a national leader; and though they never became completely that, they magnified the stature of the Prime Minister.

The power that Prime Ministers have exercised over Cabinets since 1867 had been large, difficult to define, but not unlimited. The Prime Minister owes his authority to his function of presiding over the Cabinet, of acting as intermediary between it and the monarch, and leading his party. But he has little departmental authority. His usual office of First Lord of the Treasury no longer has the significance it possessed when its command of patronage made its operation vital to the existence of any administration; and the administrative efficiency of a Cabinet must therefore depend on the Prime Minister's ability to enlist the co-operation of his colleagues. He can only hold his place as long as he is sure of a majority in the House of Commons; and if he breaks with his more important colleagues, who also stand high in the ranks of his party, he may find himself faced with a party revolt, and even forced to resign: for, in spite of his pre-eminence, a Prime Minister is not indispensable.

Once the Cabinet became organised on party lines and could appeal to the electorate through the national machinery of its party it took up a stronger position in relation to the House of Commons. It could claim that it had been returned to power in order to carry out a programme and its supporters had therefore an obligation to support it constantly; and its claim was reinforced by the growing determination of constituency parties to secure from members some deference to their wishes. After 1867 the members of the Commons had to show greater respect both to electorate and Cabinet.

Formerly Parliament had maintained a disdainful attitude to the general public. It had considered its proceedings its private concern; and it only reluctantly, after the middle of the eighteenth century, conceded the publication of its debates. Even then, the concession was grudging. No accommodation was provided for reporters until after 1834. The *Parliamentary Debates* that came to be known by the name of their publisher, Hansard, were an entirely private enterprise ⟨197⟩. But after the second Reform Act the public could not be ignored. In 1877 the government began to subsidise Hansard's *Parliamentary Debates* and in 1909 at last made it an official publication. In the same period the development of newspapers and periodicals had also exposed Parliament to the scrutiny of a wider public. After Fox's Libel Act of 1792 the press enjoyed a greater, though not always secure, freedom to comment; but for many years the expansion of newspapers was limited by the stamp and paper duties, which increased their price and restricted their circulation ⟨191⟩. By 1861 both these burdens had been removed, the price of ordinary morning newspapers fell to one penny—*The Times* to threepence—and a wide circulation could at last be achieved. In these conditions the public could not be ignored.

At the same time the back-bencher found his independence circumscribed by the ministry's increasing control over the House. By the end of the nineteenth century the ministry was reserving a great part of parliamentary time for its own business and establishing a virtual monopoly of initiating laws. New standing orders restricted the opportunities for discussion and enabled the government to limit the length of debates. Armed with such powers a ministry today, backed by a firm majority, is well equipped to perform its prime function, that of government. To this end it is important that, although dependence on party and on the electorate has allowed the government to tighten its hold over the Commons, this has not put the government, in its turn, at the constant mercy of the public in general or of its own party members outside the House. The tradition has survived—reinforced by the form of their appointment—that ministers are ministers of the crown, not just mandatories of the electorate.

Since 1867 the importance of the individual Member of Parliament has declined. Some observers would maintain that the powers of the Cabinet, the discipline of party and the increasingly technical character of governmental business, have tended progressively to reduce Parliament and

E*

particularly the ordinary Member to a cipher. This seems to be an exaggeration. The back-bencher is certainly not a mere creature of the party whip: the party machine, which communicates discipline downwards, also transmits pressure upwards to the leaders. Nor does Parliament as a whole fail to perform its most important functions. For its traditional task has not been to govern—this ambition was disavowed after the Interregnum—but rather to make government both stronger and better. From its infancy—under Edward I or Henry VIII or George III—it has had the function of enhancing the authority of the government by conferring its approval in the name of the community, thus sustaining their claim to govern. It has also had the function of acting as the watch-dog of the community, of forcing the government to justify its policies in the face of reasoned criticism. Now this second function has not, any more than the first, been undermined necessarily by the growth of party: for opposition, like government, has profited from organisation; and well-organised opposition is necessary for Parliament to perform this function effectively.

With this we arrive at the essence of parliamentary democracy in Britain. It does not only imply a system by which the electorate may from time to time change its rulers and influence their policies: it implies also a system of government by open debate and discussion. Parliament provides the forum in which the government confronts the nation, and has to make public and justify its actions. It has the character not of a public meeting but of a debating assembly where the onus is on every contributor, whether ventilating a grievance or presenting a policy, to state a reasoned case in terms of the public interest. This does not reduce Parliament to the status of an academic debating society. At the very least, even if a question in the House or vote in committee or division after debate does not immediately divert the ministry from its course, the obligation to produce a reasoned justification, the expectation of critical scrutiny, must exercise a potent, though immeasurable, influence on its formulation of policy.

*   *   *

The authority of the House of Lords evidently suffered from the progress of parliamentary reform. Once the will of the electorate had become sovereign, the House's old function in the legislative process had to be abandoned, for if it totally obstructed the popular will it stood in danger of being brushed completely aside. Indeed, the Lords could only justify their continued existence by reinterpreting their functions in democratic terms. They now claimed to serve not the rights of their order but the popular will: if they rejected a Bill that the Commons had sent up they justified their veto either because the Lower House did not adequately represent public opinion, or because the issue was so controversial that the public ought to have time for second thoughts about it. Their veto, therefore, was not to be obstructive but suspensive; and its purpose was to secure, they maintained, the true expression of opinion so as to protect the constant will of the country from its temporary whims. Under Queen Victoria they performed this function with tact and avoided, on the whole, provoking a clash with the Commons ⟨192⟩. In the early years of the twentieth century their powers led to the most severe constitutional crisis since the passing of the Great Reform Bill. Hitherto the alignment of parties in the Commons had been reflected in some degree in the Lords; and the ties of influence and family connexion had eased the relations between the two Houses. By 1906 conditions had changed. The Lords now represented overwhelmingly the Conservative Party, which was in a small minority in the Commons; and they were tempted to use their power not just to delay the passage of legislation till a cooler moment, but to support the Opposition in wrecking the government's programme. The crisis came to a head when the Lords rejected the Budget of 1909. By this they challenged the ancient and vital pre-eminence the Commons enjoyed in finance and brought into question the foundations of constitutional practice. Here the Lords had chosen their ground badly. By vetoing a Budget which imposed new taxes on landed property they opened themselves to the charge of using their powers to defend the interests of a privileged class. In 1911, after the electorate had twice decided against them, the king promised to create as many peers as might be necessary to swamp opposition in the House; and in order to avert this the Lords agreed to accept the Parliament Bill which broke their power of veto over money Bills and prevented their delaying other Bills for more than two years ⟨193⟩.

Although during this crisis the temper of public debate flamed violently the consequences were in no sense revolutionary. The Parliament Act did little more than give statutory force to the conventional limits which the Lords had generally respected after 1832; and prevented their breach. At the time the Act threatened that the Lords would be replaced by a popular revising chamber; but in fact the House has continued to perform its functions almost unchanged, except that powers of delay have been reduced since 1949 to one year. Nevertheless, as a revising chamber it still suffers from certain defects: in particular the continued predominance within it of the same party undermines public confidence in its impartiality and prevents it performing its functions adequately. Reform of the House of Lords has therefore been much discussed, but thwarted by the opposition of traditionalists, who wish to preserve the hereditary and aristocratic principle, and of radicals, who prefer an unreformed and inadequate, to a reformed and powerful, revising chamber. The only step yet taken has been to confer, since 1958, Life Peerages on eminent commoners in an attempt to improve the quality of the House.

Like the House of Lords the monarchy has survived the advent of parliamentary democracy by changing its functions. The monarch has ceased to govern: that is the responsibility of the ministers. This withdrawal of the monarch from politics had begun towards the end of the eighteenth century, but was not complete until after Queen Victoria died. By 1832 the solidarity of the Cabinet and authority of the Prime Minister had gone far to deprive the monarchy of any significant power of political decision, but its proper role in the new political order was not yet established. It was the merit of Queen Victoria's long reign to establish it. Not that Victoria always observed the political neutrality that is nowadays appropriate, for, particularly in old age, she showed a markedly Conservative bias; but on the whole her partisan interventions had little effect on policies, took place behind the scenes, and did not check the general tendency to raise the crown above party. What mattered was that she did not allow the ruler to be reduced to a cipher. She not only exercised fully her right to advise and warn her ministers, but insisted, in spite of the arduous labour involved, on being kept in touch with every detail of public business, even if it concerned only the colour of the gaiters worn by the Brigade of Guards. She ensured that the monarch remains not just a decorative but a working head of state. Today, the ruler is not likely to exert much direct influence on policy even by advice and warning; but it may not be without effect that a Prime Minister has to explain and justify his measures to his sovereign as he does to Parliament.

In ceasing to be head of the government the monarch has not ceased to be the head of the state, but rather developed the function of the crown as a symbol of national unity and focus of loyalty. Not only are the ministers servants of the crown; even their opponents are called Her Majesty's Opposition and their leader is paid from public funds. For this reason the ceremonial duties of the monarchy, though neglected for some time by Queen Victoria in the middle of her reign, have been maintained and enlarged; and the pageantry of royal occasions, reaching to a wider public than ever, continues to relieve drab workaday politics and marks, by appropriate ceremony, the most solemn moments of the nation's life ⟨198, 199, 200⟩.

*　　*　　*

As striking as the development of parliamentary democracy, and not unconnected with it, has been the expansion of the state's functions and a revolution in men's conception of what the state can and ought to do. In the past the central government had been concerned chiefly with the attributes of state power, with internal security, with foreign affairs, the armed forces and the taxation necessary to sustain it; but the pressure of social problems and social classes that could no longer be ignored forced governments, reluctantly for the most part, and often haphazardly, to take on new duties and intervene in spheres hitherto considered to be entirely a matter of private action. In some instances intervention was made necessary by technical developments which clearly required some public regulation: the railway, the motor car (see *Transport*, pp. 60–1), the aeroplane, radio, television, all created new problems and imposed new duties on the government. In other cases the increased complexity of an age-old function, like national defence, has forced the state to take on tasks, such as the development of atomic energy, that are far too dangerous and too expensive to be entrusted to private hands. Sometimes intervention was inspired by negative considerations, by the sheer need to mitigate the evident evils that arose from a growing, industrial, urban society; at other times by positive considerations, by the recognition that the collective action of the community can enhance the life of the individual.

Whatever its cause or inspiration, this expansion did not advance at a steady pace or according to a logical plan or, for the most part, at the call of doctrine. The first significant Acts of social welfare, for example, belong to the period immediately following the first Reform Act, when in other respects state intervention was extremely suspect. The Factory Act of 1833, though not in itself far-reaching—for it only regulated the employment of young children in textile manufactures—took a decisive step in introducing for the first time the device of government inspectors. This provision made it the first effective Factory Act, provided a model for subsequent wider-reaching legislation and, above all, tacitly accepted the lesson that legislation, however well-intentioned, could not achieve its objects without establishing some form of central control. The Poor Law Amendment Act of 1834 had wider implications ⟨147⟩. It tackled a bigger problem in a bigger way. It not only regulated the administration of poor relief throughout the country, but entrusted its supervision to the central government through the agency of a Poor Law Commission. The Commissioners were more than inspectors appointed to report infringements of the law: they were a governing body invested with real administrative powers and the discretion to issue orders and regulations. This Act reversed the tendencies of nearly two centuries and entrenched on the extensive autonomy that the justices of the peace had enjoyed since the destruction of conciliar government. And, like the Factory Act, it created a precedent for subsequent wider action. From the Poor Law Commission there arose in 1871 the Local Government Board, which, until 1919, provided the central government's chief instrument of public welfare. It was in this period, too, that the state first assumed some responsibility for en-couraging popular education. It was a trifling beginning when, in 1833, Parliament voted £20,000 towards the building of schools: but it led, in 1839, to the creation of an Education Committee of the Privy Council and the appointment of school inspectors; and might have had more immediate consequences if the whole development of public education had not been set back by disputes between the religious denominations.

Although these measures were the work of a Whig government such legislation was not the monopoly of a single party. It was the Conservative ministry of Peel that, by the Mines Act of 1842, not only prohibited the employment of women and girls underground, but enforced the law by providing an inspectorate such as had already proved its worth in factory legislation; and the same ministry secured in 1844 the first Factory Act to limit the working hours of adult women and to require the fencing of machinery. Even the period of party confusion between 1846 and 1859 did not stop the process; for the cause of social welfare was not funda-mentally a party matter, but forwarded rather by the nagging persistence of disinterested philanthropists like the seventh Lord Shaftesbury, or by the extra-parliamentary agitation of a public shocked by the scandals revealed in the reports of Royal Commissions. Thus this period of weak governments was responsible for the Ten Hours Act of 1847 which, in the long run, reduced the hours of work in factories for men as well as women and children: it was responsible, too, for the foundation, in 1851, of the Royal School of Mines which trained inspectors and provided the expert knowledge required for further improvements in a dangerous trade. Now also the central government at last concerned itself with the urgent prob-lem of public health, when, stirred by the report of the Commission on the Health of Towns, it set up, in 1848, a Central Board of Health on the lines of the Poor Law Commission and charged it with the duty of securing a necessary minimum of sanitary provision in the most outrageously disease-ridden areas. And even in the decade before the second Reform Act govern-ments continued to build on the precedents already established; Factory Acts were passed in 1864 and 1867 with the purpose not only of restricting the work-ing day but enforcing safe conditions. In 1860 came the first Food Adultera-tion Act, the ancestor of the host of regulations which now seek—and with difficulty as age-old ingenuity is reinforced by modern chemistry—to protect a public which has become increasingly dependent on factory-made products.

In enfranchising the urban artisan and forcing the government to pay still more attention to social problems, the second Reform Act did not immediately lead to a radical new conception of the state's role, but rather increased the pace of the march along lines already marked out. In the following half-century a number of Factory and Workshop Acts consolidated and extended earlier legislation about hours and conditions of work; and the principle of employers' liability was established before the century ended. But even the most important social measures adopted in this period did not lack precedent. The Education Act of 1870, great landmark though it was in establishing a national system of education ⟨150⟩—made free by the Conservative government in 1891—followed the hesitant precedent set earlier in the century; and the important Artisans' Dwellings Act of 1875, which for the first time empowered local authorities to carry through schemes of slum-clearance and resettlement, was not the first to establish governmental responsibility for housing. What was evident, in fact, was not a different but an increasingly broad conception of the aims of social policy as old prejudices about the limits of state action broke down over a wider front. Thus legislation designed to mitigate obvious social evils made way almost insensibly for more positive measures of social welfare and change, with the result that it is not possible to mark any precise stage at which the 'laissez-faire' state of the mid-nineteenth century ended and the so-called 'welfare' state of the mid-twentieth century began. The nearest approach to such a stage may be found in the great social legislation carried out by the Liberal government after 1906 which broke new ground with unemployment and health insurance, old age pensions and the first Town Planning Act. For these in turn prepared the way for the welfare measures introduced in 1944 and after, such as the Education Act of 1944 ⟨152⟩ and the creation of the National Health service.

The acceptance of welfare policies was made easier by the experience of two world wars, during which the government had to provide for the most ordinary necessities of life, whether by the negative means of price control and food rationing or the more positive provision of orange juice and dried milk for babies; and many of the controls established and services provided in the war were carried over into the practice of peace-time government. This was true of more than the welfare services. The requirements of war made necessary a wholesale mobilisation of economic and human resources; and this in turn prepared the way for the acceptance of economic planning and regulation in some form as a necessary responsibility of the government. Thus today a Chancellor of the Exchequer is concerned with invigorating the national economy rather than with balancing his Budget in the old sense. Since 1945, therefore, government controls have continued to proliferate, regulating foreign exchange, establishing marketing boards, or creating incentives and imposing restraints by manipulation of bank rate and purchase tax. War-time practice, also, by accustoming the country to a greater degree of state control and even operation of industry, made it easier to accept the programme of public ownership which the Labour government introduced after 1945 into transport (see *Transport*, pp. 67–8), electricity and gas, and the mines ⟨153, 154⟩. Furthermore these socialist measures appeared the less revolutionary in that they seemed in some respects to do no more than develop on a national scale public services long since provided by municipalities, many of which had supplied lighting, heating and transport facilities since well before the end of the nineteenth century.

In 1784, when the younger Pitt became Prime Minister, the annual expenditure of the government was less than £20 million a year. A hundred and seventy years later its expenditure was £4¼ thousand million, of which £1⅓ thousand million was accounted for by social services such as health, education and housing. Even when depreciation in money values is allowed for, the contrast in the scale of governmental activity is immense: yet the process of expansion, though never steady, was at no stage revolutionary.

* * *

The expansion of government business was naturally reflected in the growth of the executive departments ⟨187, 188⟩. Here, as in the constitution generally, development was a matter of piecemeal change rather than radical reorganisation. Old offices were given extended or new attributes, new departments were fitted into the general pattern of administration that had been developed by the end of the eighteenth century. The office of the Lord Chancellor extended its control over judicial appointments and acquired something like the functions of a Ministry of Justice. The office of Secretary of State, which had its origin in the post of King's Secretary and first acquired ministerial status in the sixteenth century, divided into a number of separate departments, with the creation, for example, in 1782 of separate Secretaries of State for the Home Department and for Foreign Affairs, and in 1794 of the Secretary of State for War. The office of Lord High Admiral had provided the basis for the modern Admiralty Board as long ago as the seventeenth century when its powers had been entrusted to a Commission of Lords of the Admiralty, composed partly of civilian ministers, partly of serving naval officers; and this Board provided the model for the Army Council and Air Council which now administer the other fighting services. The Treasury had its origin in the private office of the Lord Treasurer: after the beginning of the eighteenth century its powers were regularly entrusted to a Board of Commissioners known as the Lords of the Treasury and it emerged as an independent department of state with general control over financial policy; and already, at the end of the century, the real head of the department was the Chancellor of the Exchequer in his capacity of second Lord of the Treasury. Even the Exchequer survived, at least in name; for, when the ancient department was abolished in the long-overdue reorganisation of 1834, its accounting functions were transferred eventually to a new Exchequer and Audit department, under the command of an independent Comptroller and Auditor-General. The present structure of central administration appears therefore an odd assortment of historic and modern departments without an entirely logical distribution of functions among them. The Home Office, for example, though responsible above all for law and order, performs also a variety of other rather miscellaneous functions; and, as an odd historical survival, the function of censoring plays—but not films—is still vested in an officer of the royal household, the Lord Chamberlain.

Although this administrative scheme lacks an obvious pattern, it has acquired some unity from the principle of Treasury control. Even from its infancy the Treasury attempted to regulate the spending of other departments, and in the nineteenth century its control was consolidated and extended over every detail of expenditure. Through this the Treasury could also exercise a considerable control over policy; and it is this department, therefore, which provides such co-ordination as the system possesses apart from the Cabinet.

Another development that has characterised this expansion has been the acquisition by the executive of semi-legislative powers. Parliament, having deprived the monarch of his discretionary powers, found it necessary to restore them to some extent by statute. As long ago as 1689 the Mutiny Act empowered the king to lay down and enforce such military regulations as he thought necessary to maintain discipline in the army. Since 1832 such powers have been widely delegated to departments; and much of the detailed regulation of poor relief, public health, factory inspection or education was enforced by means of statutory instruments issued at departmental discretion rather than directly by parliamentary enactment. Two world wars necessarily increased the administration's reliance on such powers and such is the technical complexity of business that it has not been possible to dispense with them in time of peace.

The extent of these delegated powers has caused concern that the role of Parliament is being usurped. It can be argued, however, that Parliament still remains the supreme authority; that without these devices it would be overburdened with detailed legislation for which it is not well equipped, and that such orders are still subject to the ultimate review of the courts.

For similar reasons the executive has also acquired judicial powers. The application of new policies raised issues which the ordinary courts did not seem competent or sufficiently speedy to decide. Thus, in many cases of conflict between the citizens and the authorities, the case is heard by a departmental tribunal, as in matters relating to income tax, or social services such as pensions. Such tribunals have proliferated without any coherent plan and vary considerably in their composition and procedure. Their extent has caused concern that the rule of law and the authority of the ordinary courts is being undermined. In 1958 some of the criticisms were met by the Tribunals and Enquiries Act, which attempted to secure the ultimate authority of the ordinary courts and provide some reform of procedure: but it seems most unlikely that administrative tribunals could now be easily dispensed with.

The new character acquired by the state since 1832 also required a change in local government: it had to be made more democratic, more efficient, and brought into closer relationship with the central administration. It was important that there existed so strong a tradition of local self-government. In some other countries the problems of modern society were met by a policy of centralisation. This did not happen in Britain: although centralised control has steadily extended, this has not been entirely at the expense of local activity. In general the principle of government action has been that of central supervision but local performance. In education, for example, the Ministry does not build or operate schools nor prescribe textbooks or syllabus: it is the local authorities who run the schools but under the general supervision of the Ministry; and the same principle is applied in other functions such as the police, public health or child care. Much of the control that the central administration exercises is derived from its financial powers. Local authorities were encouraged in the first place to establish services by government 'grants in aid'; and such grants could only be continued so long as the service provided came up to the standards laid down by the appropriate ministry. This system has made it possible to achieve the necessary degree of national integration while preserving flexibility and respecting local initiative and interests.

The first attempt to reorganise local government was made in 1835— two years earlier in Scotland—by the Municipal Corporations Act. This replaced the varied traditional constitutions of 178 boroughs by a uniform system providing for a town council elected by the ratepayers. But, although this Act was important in destroying the old oligarchies and providing the model that was later to be applied also to the counties, it did not immediately reinvigorate local government in the towns. The new councils were inspired by a sense of economy rather than of public service; and they were therefore slow to attempt even the most elementary forms of municipal improvement. In consequence both in boroughs and counties new functions tended to require the creation of new and distinct authorities. Thus after 1834 the poor law was administered locally by elected guardians, not by the justices of the peace or town councils: after 1848 sanitary services were attributed to new local Boards of Health and after 1870 education was entrusted to School Boards.

This multiplication of local bodies made necessary a reorganisation which established the system still operating today. In 1888 democratic self-government was introduced into the counties when most of the administrative functions of the justices of the peace were transferred to county councils, organised and elected in much the same way as the municipal councils; and in 1894 these administrative counties were subdivided into urban and rural districts. These measures created a much simpler as well as more democratic system. The county, or municipality, now became the main instrument of local government, invested with the powers hitherto distributed among many separate agencies; and subsequent legislation, like the Education Act of 1902 which transferred the functions of the School Boards to the local councils, has only tended to reinforce its position.

On account of its size London has always presented a special problem. It had long since grown far outside the limits of the medieval city and the old corporation to form a great urban area administered in a haphazard fashion by a large number of districts and parishes. In 1888 the problem was tackled, the administrative County of London formed, and the government of the whole area vested in an elective county council. Shortly afterwards the lesser local authorities were reorganised into twenty-eight metropolitan boroughs—a reorganisation, however, which respected old boundaries and even preserved the ancient city corporation.

In the last thirty years the simple pattern of local government established after 1888 has been modified by demands of efficiency, which favour larger units of administration. For this reason some services have been transferred from local to central authorities, as with trunk roads and motorways, unemployment assistance; or to regional authorities, as with hospitals. Even the L.C.C., no longer thought competent, in spite of its size, to serve the needs of Greater London, lies under sentence of death.

Many important public duties and services are carried out by bodies that do not form an integral part of the machinery of government, such as the British Broadcasting Corporation, the Port of London Authority, the National Coal Board or the Forestry Commission. In order to secure commercial efficiency or freedom from political pressure such bodies enjoy some independence of parliamentary control and are not directly subject to any ministry. The device is not new—the Mersey Docks and Harbour Board was established in 1857—but its use has been greatly extended in recent times with the creation of Marketing Boards and the nationalisation of certain industries and services.

One of the great achievements of nineteenth-century reformers was to create a professional civil service standing outside politics, highly qualified, and equipped to provide the expert advice and administrative continuity that the parliamentary system lacks. Since 1784 the younger Pitt had been gradually purging the administrative service of the most notorious sinecures and replacing them by effective, working, offices; and this process in itself went far towards eliminating the worst abuses by which offices had been traded for votes. It did not, however, go far enough; for patronage still played a large part in deciding appointments and, as no uniform qualifications were required, there was no guarantee that considerations of aptitude and efficiency would prevail. It was not until 1853 that the Trevelyan-Northcote Report recommended the principles on which recruitment to the civil service is now based: admission by competitive examination; division into higher and lower grades according to the qualifications required; unification into one single, uniformly regulated, service. And, although Civil Service Commissioners were appointed in 1855 to conduct examinations, the principles of the report were not effectively adopted until 1870 and not applied to the Foreign Service until 1943.

Without these changes the service would hardly have been competent to handle the growing and increasingly complex business of government. Much of the responsibility for the achievements of the last hundred years must lie with the comparatively small administrative class of civil servants —now numbering about 3,000—who, with the ministers, really control the central departments. The criticism is frequently made that these higher civil servants are not drawn from sufficiently wide social classes; but at least the common social and academic background that they have usually shared with the ministers they serve has helped in the past to create harmony between them and to establish the standards of loyalty and integrity that have distinguished the service. It would be a more pertinent criticism that the standards and uniformity of the civil service have not been applied to the administration of local government. For although local authorities, like the central government, have had to create an extensive staff of permanent officials and have enlisted many men of ability, the respect for local autonomy has prevented them from achieving all the advantage that might accrue from a unified service.

*   *   *

Before the nineteenth century the resources of public order were slight, consisting for the most part of parish constables and the watch ⟨156⟩. The difficulty of maintaining order in London had led in the eighteenth century to the introduction of professional forces like the Bow Street Runners; but the Gordon Riots of 1780 revealed how easily the 'mob' could get out of hand ⟨155, 157⟩. The first thorough-going attempt to provide a solution had the merit of success: this was Peel's Act of 1829 which established the Metropolitan Police ⟨158⟩. This succeeded so well that it provided a model for the rest of the country, with this exception, that the Metropolitan Police was directly controlled—and is still—by the Home Office. It was only after 1839 that local authorities were encouraged to establish their own police forces, and not until 1856 that such forces were established throughout the country and subjected to the inspection of the Home Office. With the successful introduction of the police the public order that is the necessary foundation of civilised life was for the first time secured.

Justice has always been one of the essential functions of government and its administration one of the tests of good government. At the beginning of the nineteenth century its administration in England suffered from serious defects; for the procedure and complexity of the courts made justice uncertain, slow and expensive. The vested interests involved and the conservatism of the legal profession long delayed the necessary reforms. The creation of County Courts in 1846 relieved the pressure a little; but thorough reorganisation had to wait until the Judicature Act of 1873. This was a great act of simplification. It abolished the old distinction between common law and equity, fusing the two. It united the old Common Law Courts with Chancery and other central courts, like the Court of Admiralty, into a single Supreme Court of Judicature sitting, eventually, in three divisions ⟨160⟩. It provided what had always been lacking under the old order, an effective Court of Appeal. Respect for tradition, however, prevented this being a final Court of Appeal; and an Act of 1876 maintained the ancient right of the House of Lords. This was characteristic of the reform of the law in general. It respected the traditional features of the English judicial system such as the centralisation of the courts and the independence of the legal profession. But in spite of recent developments like free legal aid, justice is still not a cheap commodity.

The test of a government's quality lies in its treatment not only of the good but the bad citizen. Before the nineteenth century resources were too slight and the philosophy of crime and punishment too little considered for the treatment of offenders to be anything but rough and haphazard. Minor offences usually earned corporal penalties such as whipping or being put in the stocks, the pillory ⟨168⟩ or—in the case of scolding women—the ducking stool ⟨26⟩. Major offences were punished by fines or branding ⟨169⟩, banishment or death. By the eighteenth century branding and banishment had fallen into disuse; transportation to the colonies had been introduced ⟨172⟩; and the death penalty applied to an increasing number of crimes, over 200 in all. Hanging then was the common sentence for crimes against property and the theft of as little as 5s. from a shop could bring a man—or child—to the gallows. The time came, however, when these penal methods ceased to be acceptable to civilised opinion. Humanitarians found the penalties barbarous and the ancient practice of public hangings and exposure on the gibbet degrading. Others were scandalised at the inefficiency which tempered the inhumanity of these methods; for, when penalties were so extreme, juries frequently refused to convict. And so, after 1823, the work of penal reform began—later than in many other European countries. Public whippings, the pillory and the like were abolished: transportation ceased to be common after 1852; and by 1861 capital offences were reduced to four, remaining at that number until the Homicide Act of 1957.

Penal reform had to be accompanied by prison reform; for it changed the purpose that prisons served. For the most part imprisonment had not been a punishment or a means of reforming offenders: the common jails had merely been places in which accused persons could be held securely until tried. Some change had been introduced by Elizabeth and the early Stuarts who had imposed imprisonment as a punishment for minor offences like vagrancy, for debt and non-payment of fines; and had empowered local authorities to build Bridewells and Houses of Correction for the purpose. However this did not greatly alter the general character of English prisons: they were mostly places of temporary incarceration, the building and management of which were thought to require no special care. A prison might be a small lock-up ⟨162⟩, or an underground room in a castle or a cellar. Whether owned privately or by a local authority its management was farmed out, the jailer paying a rent for it and recouping himself from fees to be paid by the prisoners. In consequence prisons were quite ill-equipped for the new functions attributed to them. The rigour of imprisonment depended on the whims of the jailers and the size of the prisoner's purse. The indiscriminate mingling of first offenders and hardened criminals made prisons schools of crime, and exposed their inmates to demoralisation as well as jail fever and other diseases bred by the prevalent filth.

If imprisonment was to punish and reform adequately there had to be sanitation, segregation, accommodation in cells and greater security; there had to be a paid staff and a uniform standard of treatment. John Howard, who published his *State of the Prisons* in 1777, succeeded by his agitation in improving the sanitary state of the prisons; but the other abuses remained and in prison reform as in penal reform England lagged behind the Continent. The first effective step was taken in 1835 when the Home Office was empowered to lay down minimum standards for all prisons and appoint inspectors to enforce them; and in 1877 the state took over the ownership of prisons and entrusted their administration to Prison Commissioners acting under the authority of the Home Secretary ⟨164, 165⟩.

Since that time reform has taken several lines. Acts of 1898 and 1948 humanised the harsh, drab routine of Victorian prisons with their crank machines, treadmills ⟨171⟩ and silence, and enabled treatment to be adjusted to suit the particular offender. Since 1936 experiments have been made

68

with 'open prisons' in order to improve the chances of rehabilitation. Other measures have provided alternatives to imprisonment. Imprisonment for debt was abolished, longer periods allowed for paying fines, and probation introduced. Special provision was made for children and young offenders. Victorian philanthropists, like Shaftesbury, had, by voluntary effort, established reformatory and industrial schools to which children and youths could be sent instead of prison. As early as 1854 such schools received official approval, and later the authorities established their own; but it is worthy of note that about half of these 'approved schools' are still maintained by voluntary societies ⟨167⟩. In 1908 imprisonment of children under the age of fourteen was prohibited, juvenile courts were established and Borstals introduced for youths ⟨166⟩; and these measures were reinforced in 1938. Partly by these means prison population remains the smallest, in relation to total population, of any country of western Europe.

*   *   *

The history of social reform in the past 150 years throws some light on the character of English government. To understand it one must look beyond the formal apparatus of the ballot box, party, Parliament and Cabinet. For much of the achievement was the work not directly of party or the electorate but of enlightened civil servants, societies or private citizens who agitated and organised public opinion to bring pressure on the government. No attempt to understand how policies are formulated and decisions made can exclude the influence of such 'pressure groups', whether formal or informal. Nowadays almost every possible cause has some association to protect or advance its interests. Furthermore many associations not only help to mobilise opinion and put pressure on government but give practical and, in some cases, indispensable service to the public.

The readiness to pay attention to organised opinion, the reluctance to offend vested interests or uproot established rights, the preference for voluntary co-operation, the prejudice in favour of local opinion and variety at the expense of uniformity, accounts for some of the virtues of the English tradition of government and for some of its vices. It accounts for the difficulty of carrying through necessary improvements—even to construct a motorway requires years of negotiation—so that English government can hardly be counted among the most efficient, if results achieved are related to the effort expended. Yet it also illustrates the tolerance and lack of dogmatism which have made it possible to perform the prime function of government—that of containing the conflicts and contentions of society within peaceful political limits and adjusting methods to suit changing conditions.

Bibliographical Note

So many books have been written about British government that every paragraph of this introduction could well have a bibliography to itself. Here, therefore, space permits nothing more than an attempt to indicate fuller bibliographical sources and mention a somewhat arbitrary selection of individual books, chosen as classics in their field, or as useful introductions, or as recent studies that might not yet be listed elsewhere.

For further bibliographical information consult S. B. Chrimes and I. A. Roots, *English Constitutional History: A Select Bibliography* (1958, No. 58 in the series *Helps for Students of History*, published by the Historical Association), and J. Palmer, *Government and Parliament in Britain: A Bibliography* (1960, Hansard Society). The volumes in the *Oxford History of England* contain comprehensive critical bibliographies in addition to their valuable pages on the history of government. The series *English Historical Documents* also contains useful commentaries and bibliographies.

S. B. Chrimes, *English Constitutional History* (2nd ed. 1953), provides a concise introduction to the whole subject. D. L. Keir, *The Constitutional History of Modern Britain* (5th ed. 1953), though dated in parts, is the most useful single volume of any substance on the period since 1485. The most comprehensive survey is given by W. S. Holdsworth, *A History of English Law* (vol. 1 rev. ed. 1956, vols. 2–3 3rd ed. 1922–3, vols. 4–13 1924–52), a classic which covers a much wider field than its title suggests and, for all its bulk, achieves the rare distinction of a value commensurate with its size. T. F. T. Plucknett, *A Concise History of the Common Law* (5th ed. 1956), achieves his purpose with characteristic lucidity. P. E. Schramm, *A History of the English Coronation* (1937), traces with imaginative insight the attitudes to monarchy reflected in the changing forms of the coronation order.

For the medieval period a scholarly, critical and sometimes controversial study of the foundations of English government will be found in H. E. Richardson and G. O. Sayles, *The Governance of Medieval England from the Conquest to Magna Carta* (1963). For introductory purposes G. W. S. Barrow, *Feudal Britain* (1956), has the merit of surveying Scotland and Wales in addition to England, and C. Brooke, *From Alfred to Henry III* (1061), and G. Holmes, *The Later Middle Ages* (1962), succinctly sum up recent scholarship. The early history of Parliament defies a definite statement, but some judicious guidance may be found in T. F. T. Plucknett's chapter in *The English Government at Work, 1327–36*, vol. 1, ed. J. F. Willard and W. A. Morris (1940). Miss M. McKisack traces an important aspect of parliamentary development in *The Parliamentary Representation of the English Boroughs during the Middle Ages* (1932). Administrative history is well served by S. B. Chrimes, *An Introduction to the Administrative History of Medieval England* (2nd. ed. 1958), and T. F. Tout's *Chapters in the Administrative History of Medieval England* (6 vols. 1920–33), a *magnum opus* in more senses than one, which gave a new direction to the study of the medieval constitution.

Indispensable for the early modern period are J. E. Neale's *The Elizabethan House of Commons* (1949) and *Elizabeth I and her Parliaments* (2 vols. 1953–7). In *The Structure of Politics at the Accession of George III* (rev. ed. 1957) L. B. Namier introduced into the analysis of politics a revolution that has extended far beyond the limits of the original study. Two useful introductory works are G. R. Elton, *The Tudor Constitution. Documents and Commentary* (1953), and the companion volume on *The Eighteenth Century Constitution* by E. N. Williams (1960). The administrative history of this period has been the subject of some interesting recent studies. The most important, but also the most controversial, is G. R. Elton, *The Tudor Revolution in Government* (1953), which discovers, with exaggerated determination to state a case, an administrative revolution in Henry VIII's reign and attributes it to Thomas Cromwell. W. C. Richardson, *History of the Court of Augmentations 1536–1554* (1961), and H. E. Bell, *An Introduction to the history and records of the Court of Wards and Liveries* (1953), give sober accounts of particular aspects of Tudor financial administration. Some of the difficulties in the way of administrative reform are explained by G. E. Aylmer, *The King's Servants: the Civil Service of Charles I 1625–42* (1961). For the study of local government the great work of S. and B. Webb, *English Local Government from the Revolution to the Municipal Corporations Act* (9 vols. 1900–29), remains fundamental. L. Radzinowicz, *A History of English Criminal Law and its administration from 1750* (3 vols. 1948–56), provides a thorough examination of law enforcement just before the great age of penal reform.

A useful guide to the making of the modern constitution is provided by K. B. Smellie, *A Hundred Years of English Government* (rev. ed. 1950). A. V. Dicey's *Lectures on the Relation between Law and Public Opinion during the Nineteenth Century* (1905) remain an illuminating analysis of the motives and principles behind the great reforms of the century, although his distinction between the phases of individualism and collectivism now appears too simple and clear-cut. W. Bagehot, *The English Constitution* (rev. ed. 1877), ought to be read as the starting point of modern discussion, with its distinction between the 'dignified' and 'efficient' elements in government. Another classic, which did much to determine the course of subsequent inquiry, is A. V. Dicey's *Introduction to the Study of the Law of the Constitution* (10th ed. 1950). An admirably clear account of the present-day organisation of government will be found in *Britain: an Official Handbook, 1960*, published by the Central Office of Information, chapters of which (e.g. *Government and Administration of the United Kingdom*) are also published separately. A more critical recent introduction to the modern constitution is given by G. C. Moodie, *The Government of Great Britain* (1961). J. P. Mackintosh, *The British Cabinet* (1962), provides a useful examination of a central institution. Valuable reflections on government by practising politicians are rare; hence the particular importance to be attached to L. S. Amery's *Thoughts on the Constitution* (1947) and H. Morrison's *Government and Parliament* (1954). Some of the difficulties relating to the modern constitution are considered by G. Marshall and G. C. Moodie, *Some Problems of the Constitution* (1959).

For the development of Scottish institutions *A Source Book of Scottish History*, ed. W. C. Dickinson, G. Donaldson and I. A. Milne (3 vols. 1952–4), is useful. An up-to-date outline and bibliographies are offered by W. C. Dickinson, *Scotland from the Earliest Times to 1603* (1961), and G. S. Pryde, *Scotland from 1603 to the Present Day* (1962). R. L. G. Ritchie, *The Normans in Scotland* (1954), studies the formative period of the Scottish kingdom and P. Hume Brown, *The Legislative Union of England and Scotland* (1914), describes the end of the Scottish parliament. An account of the present administration of Scotland is given in the *Handbook on Scottish Administration* (1956), published by Her Majesty's Stationery Office.

The student of Welsh history is well served by *A Bibliography of the History of Wales*, ed. History and Law Committee of the Board of Celtic Studies of the University of Wales (1962), though it is too comprehensive and uncritical for introductory purposes. J. E. Lloyd, *A History of Wales from the Earliest Times to the Edwardian Conquest* (3rd. ed. 2 vols. 1939), is a masterly exposition but stronger on politics than institutions. A. H. Williams, *An Introduction to the History of Wales* (2 vols. 1948–9), is clear and concise, but unfortunately stops at 1284. J. G. Edwards, 'The Normans and the Welsh March', *Proceedings of the British Academy*, xlii (1956), and J. R. Morris, *The Welsh Wars of Edward I* (1901), illuminate important aspects of Welsh history. Post-conquest Wales lacks a substantial general history: for an introduction consult D. Williams, *A History of Modern Wales* (1950). William Rees, *South Wales and the March, 1284–1415* (1924), considers primarily social and agrarian history but has a section on administration. An account of the present administration of Wales will be found in *Government and Administration in Wales* (Cmnd. 631, 1959), published by Her Majesty's Stationery Office.

ES:

ḢIC DEDERVNT:ḢAROLDO: ḢIC RE SIDET:ḢAROLD

CORO NÃ: REGIS REX:AN GLORVM:

STIGANT

ARCḢI EPS

1 The majesty of the English monarchy was already established before the Norman Conquest. Harold II, last of the Anglo-Saxon kings, here sits enthroned after his coronation in 1066. The scene on the left may represent the traditional formality of electing a king. The tonsured ecclesiastic is Stigand, Archbishop of Canterbury, who presents the king to the people. Harold holds the sceptre, symbol of his power as ruler, and the orb surmounted by a cross, symbolising the world dominated by Christianity. These insignia of royalty express not only the king's authority but the spiritual sanctions that support it.

2 A medieval coronation. This illumination, which stresses the king's devotion to the Church, purports to depict the coronation of Henry III. It shows the king being presented to the people at the end of the ceremony. The ritual was much as it was before the Conquest. The traditional coronation vestments, consisting of the long silk tunic, the buskins and sandals, the stole and royal mantle, seemed, like the rite of consecration, to emphasise the king's affinity with the priesthood.

3 The coronation of Henry VI in 1429. By this date the ceremony had reached its fullest development; but this occasion presents unusual features, presumably necessary because the king was only a child. He wears his parliament robes, not the traditional vestments; he is not seated on the coronation chair, and two bishops appear to be supporting the weight of the crown. The drawing seems to show the moment after the enthronement, when the peers stand round the king and offer him fealty.

4 The Ampulla and Spoon, alone among the medieval regalia, survived the Interregnum. At the consecration, the holy oil is poured from the beak of the golden eagle into the coronation spoon for the anointing. In the later Middle Ages the king was also anointed with the still more holy chrism, a distinction shared only with the French king. Only these two rulers were therefore reputed to have the power to cure scrofula, the king's evil. Although chrism ceased to be used after the Reformation the ceremony of touching for the king's evil continued until 1714.

5 A writ of William I to the citizens of London, 1067. The Norman Conquest did not break the continuity of government. In this document the king promises that he will respect the rights London had enjoyed under Edward the Confessor. The language used is Anglo-Saxon, not Norman-French. The writ itself was an English, not a Norman invention, a businesslike instrument far more efficient than anything used elsewhere in Europe. Here then we see the Conqueror, who in Normandy had no chancery, no seal and kept few records, adopting English methods of administration.

6 Domesday Book has been called the 'greatest and oldest of all our public records'. It is nothing less than a comprehensive survey of the landed property of England and of those who held it, ordered by William I in 1085 and carried out with such energy that it was probably finished when he died in 1087. This meticulous and searching inquisition made so formidable an impression that the popular imagination could find nothing to compare with it except the Last Judgment or Day of Doom. From the first it enjoyed an immense authority and for four hundred years was constantly consulted in the Exchequer by both officials and private persons. Today it remains not only a historical record of the first importance but an impressive testimony to the vigour of Anglo-Norman government. It occupies two volumes, the larger of which is shown here, lying open at the entries relating to Gloucestershire,

7 The feudal relationship both strengthened and limited the king's power. It bound the vassal to perform specific services to his lord; but it also bound the king to observe his part of the contract, to respect the rights of his vassal. In effect it established a constitutional relationship. This illustration, *above left*, from the Register of the Honour of Richmond, was made in the fifteenth century, when the feudal bond had lost much of its meaning; but it conveys the concept well. It purports to show William I holding up a conveniently stiff charter by which he grants to his nephew, Alan, Earl of Brittany, the lands and rights of the Saxon Edwin. Alan kneels before the king and offers obedience.

8 *Above right:* An *inspeximus* or confirmation of Magna Carta by Edward III.

8a Magna Carta, *below*, granted by King John in 1215, was to a great extent a feudal document. It was intended by the barons to provide a written and official definition of their rights and obligations; it was made necessary by the inability of the old unwritten customs to protect them from royal encroachments. John's successors were obliged to confirm the Charter and by the end of the thirteenth century it had acquired the status of a fundamental constitutional document. When Edward I confirmed it in 1297 it was appropriate that it should be recorded on the new roll, the Statute Roll, that Chancery had recently opened for documents of special public significance. It is this enrolment which is illustrated here.

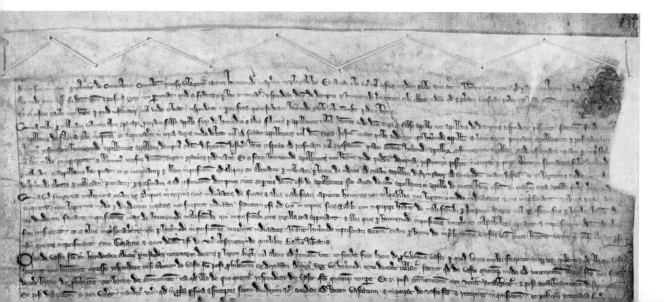

9, 10 The chief purpose of a seal was to authenticate a document: in an illiterate society it held the place of the modern signature. A royal seal existed in England before the Conquest and it seems to have provided the model for the Great Seal of William I. It has been said that 'for centuries the history of Executive Government in this Country is a history of Seals'. The growth of business required additional seals and round the seals grew administrative departments. *Above left:* The Great Seal of Henry VI: the Great Seal was two-sided and this is the obverse, the side intended to lie uppermost. *Above right:* The seal of Edward, Earl of Rutland and Cork, Admiral of England in 1397. *Below right:* The Privy Seal of Richard II. This is the first of his reign, being applied to a Warrant for Issue dated March 1378, addressed to William Walworth and John Philipot, Receivers of money for the French war. Walworth and Philipot were both important merchants of London. Walworth was the Lord Mayor who slew Wat Tyler. *Below left:* A signet of Richard II. This bears the word 'richard' between two triangles. Subsequent signets have borne the royal arms.

12 The Exchequer took its name from the chequered cloth which covered the audit table and was used with counters for calculation. It is shown here in 1811 during the presentation of the sheriffs of London to the Cursitor Baron, standing in the foreground. On the table are six horseshoes, 61 hobnails, a billhook and hatchet, with two sticks cut to prove the quality of the blades: these are services rendered for lands which the Londoners held of the king. No one now knew what lands they were, but the services continued to be exacted.

11 Exchequer tallies provided an elementary form of receipt. The tally was a stick, eight inches long, appropriately notched to represent pounds, shillings and pence, and split to form matching halves, known as the stock and foil. The stock was kept by the person making payment and the foil remained in the Exchequer. The topmost tally shown here has four notches, each representing a score of pounds, cut on its lower edge, and five, each representing one pound, on the upper edge. Tallies continued to be cut until 1826. When, in 1834, the Exchequer of Receipt was abolished the old tallies were burned; and the Houses of Parliament were consumed with them.

13, 14 The maintenance of regular written records marks an important stage in the development of government. The Exchequer appears to have been a pioneer in this. Here, *above*, is the earliest of such records that is known to survive. It is the Pipe Roll of 1129–30. It records the royal dues for which the sheriff of each shire had to account to the Exchequer: the membrane illustrated relates to Surrey. Each membrane was known as a *pipa*; and a number of membranes tied together at the head formed a roll — hence Pipe Roll. But the continuity that written records make possible has its drawbacks: it leads to the prolongation of old forms when the need for them has passed. Seven hundred years later the last Pipe Roll, *below*, maintained the ancient form, except that it was kept in English: even Roman numerals were still used. Yet by 1833, the year of this account, the ancient dues or 'farm' of the shire, once the mainstay of royal finance, formed a trifling part of the national revenue; and the Pipe Roll had lost all real significance.

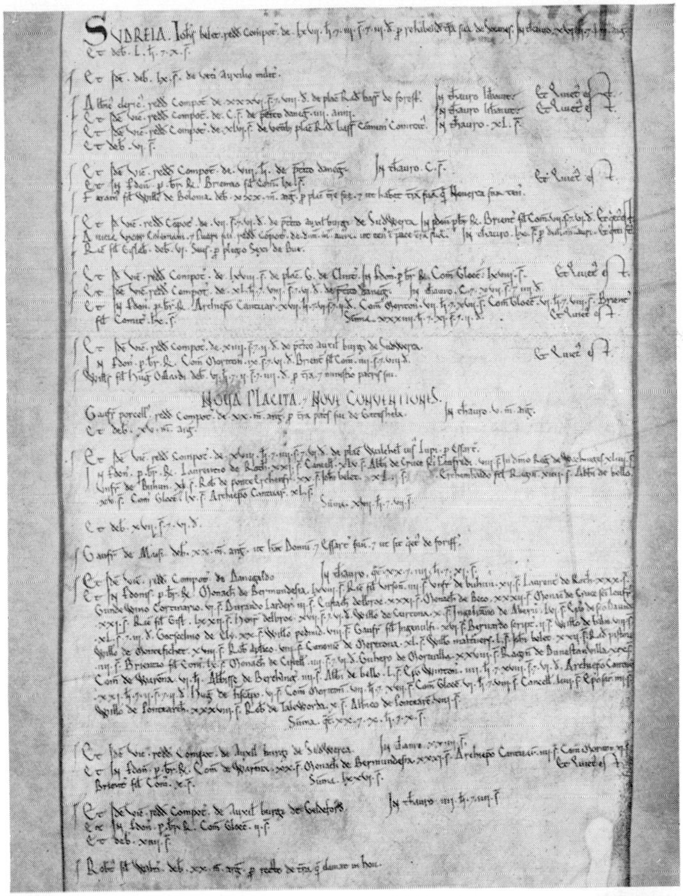

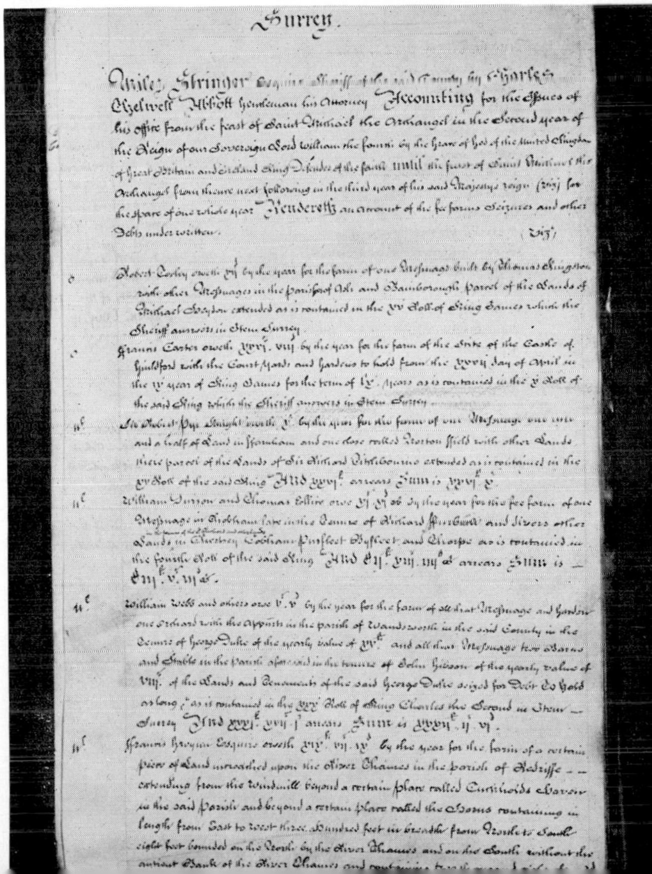

15 This faint picture, drawn in 1249 above the relevant judicial report, provides a unique illustration of a judicial combat or trial by battle, a procedure recognised by law until 1818. It shows two men engaged in such a combat. Their names, Walter Bloweberme and Hamon le Stare, are written above. Walter had accused Hamon of theft: Hamon denied it; and each claimed the right to prove his cause in battle. Hamon's defeat proved his guilt. The drawing on the left shows him on the gallows.

16 This eleventh-century drawing of a king doing justice in person assisted by his counsellors belongs to a comparatively primitive stage in the development of government. But even when, after the twelfth century, the bulk of the crown's judicial functions had devolved upon the judges of the common-law courts the King's Council could still do justice by virtue of the judicial supremacy vested in the king. A vestige of that power survives in the royal prerogative of mercy and in the functions of the Judicial Committee of the Privy Council.

17, 18 Two places with a continuous history as centres of government from Norman times to the present. *Right:* the Castle and County Hall, Chester, from an eighteenth-century water-colour. As the county acquired the status of a palatinate Chester became a miniature capital with its Exchequer, Chancery and courts of law under a Justice of Chester. It did not receive parliamentary representation or J.P.s until Henry VIII's reign, when its Exchequer lost its financial functions. The palatine courts functioned until 1830 and the Castle continued to serve as the county gaol. The façade of the County Hall, on the left (demolished in 1790), covers the hall built by the first Norman Earl. The courts are still held on the same site. *Below:* The interior of the great Norman Hall of Oakham Castle, in which the assizes of Rutland have been held since the thirteenth century.

19, 20 The four courts of justice at Westminster in the fifteenth century. *Left:* King's Bench: the chained prisoners who stand haplessly in the foreground in charge of tipstaffs show that it is a court of criminal jurisdiction. The five judges wear scarlet robes, lined and trimmed with white. The wig was not introduced until the seventeenth century: here the judges wear the coif, a white linen cap worn by all serjeants at law, a superior order of barristers from which Common Law judges were always chosen until 1873. Officials of the court sit below the judges. In front of them is a table covered with a green cloth. Two ushers stand on it. One of them administers an oath on a bible to the jury. A prisoner stands between counsel, guarded by a tipstaff. *Right:* Common Pleas, or court of civil jurisdiction, shown here without a jury and with a defendant who, though in the custody of a tipstaff and clad only in his shirt, is at least not chained. At this time it was distinguished by having seven judges. Below the picture of the court, which is taken from a legal treatise, may be seen the beginning of a list of the book's contents.

21, 22 *Left:* The Court of Exchequer. The presiding judge wears scarlet, his fellow Barons yellow robes. Three of them wear large turban-like hoods but the other two wear the coif and hold their hoods in their hands. The table is not covered with a chequered cloth, perhaps because the occasion is not an audit; but clerks are counting money on it. In the foreground appears, in odd perspective, a cage occupied by two prisoners: near it, on the floor, lie two treasure chests, bound with iron. *Right:* The Court of Chancery. As befits a court of equity or conscience the judges are evidently, from their tonsures, ecclesiastics. An exception may be the Chancellor in the centre, for he wears a cap. If, unusually at this time, he is a layman he must be Richard Neville, Earl of Salisbury, who was Chancellor from 1454 to 1455. The Chancellor and the Master of the Rolls, who holds up a document with pendant great seal, wear red robes, the other judges yellow. On the table lie a number of writs folded up, with pendant labels, the form in which Chancery writs used to be prepared until the nineteenth century. On their right a clerk or sealer uses a roller to press down the matrix of the great seal on the wax attached to a document that lies open on the table.

Neustria Johis sut in defensa sub annis
Om qp deliquit gallis possessa reliquit

Johannes Rex genuit videlicet

Henricum
Regem
Anglie.

23 To protect their sport, medieval kings declared large tracts of land—at one time almost a third of the country—royal forest, subject to special laws which imposed irksome restrictions, enforced by forest courts and heavy penalties. The harsh administration of forest law led to remedial clauses being inserted in Magna Carta and afterwards in a separate Charter of the Forest. Charles I, in need of revenue, tried to revive the now much depleted forests; but after 1640 they lost their significance.

24 Ecclesiastical privilege presented the greatest obstacle to royal justice. The quarrel between Henry II and Thomas Becket arose in part over the Archbishop's claim that the secular courts had no jurisdiction over the clergy, even in cases of theft and murder. The martyrdom of Becket in 1170, illustrated here from a nearly contemporary MS, so shocked Europe that Henry had to give way. As the penalties that the church courts imposed were not capable of disciplining a carelessly recruited profession, benefit of clergy remained an affront to public order until remedied by the Tudors.

25 This early twelfth-century sanctuary knocker that glares from the main door of Durham Cathedral is not just an ornament. Its grotesque head, with eyes originally gleaming with crystal or enamel, expressed the power of the sanctuary that it offered and the curse that would fall on those who violated it. The right of sanctuary provides an obvious example of the medieval liberties which complicated enforcement of the law. In 1540 Henry VIII imposed drastic limits on it; in 1623 the right was abolished by statute.

26 This early sixteenth-century carving shows a woman being carried in a wheelbarrow to a ducking-stool. This was a punishment commonly used for scolds and sometimes for dishonest tradesmen. Until the nineteenth century the ducking-stool remained with the stocks, whipping-post and pillory a normal feature of the village scene.

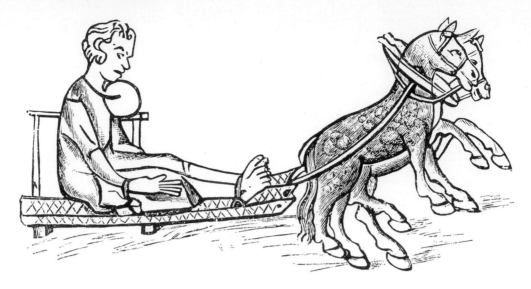

27 This drawing, based on one dating from the reign of Edward I, shows a baker found guilty of short weight drawn in a sledge to the pillory with the faulty loaf tied round his neck. Bread, like ale, was a staple commodity and therefore the subject of much regulation. The assizes of bread and ale fixed the weight of the loaf and the price of the gallon of ale according to the price of grain; and the enforcement of these assizes was a constant object of concern for local authorities.

28 The first surviving record of the presence of the Commons in a properly constituted parliament. The lower document is a writ of summons to the first parliament of Edward I. It is addressed to the sheriff of Middlesex, dated at Woodstock 26 Dec. 1274, ordering him to send to London four knights of the shire and six or four citizens, burgesses and other honest men from each of the cities, boroughs and trading towns of his bailiwick. Above is a writ addressed to the sheriff of Kent for the parliament of October 1275 ordering him to send knights of the shire only.

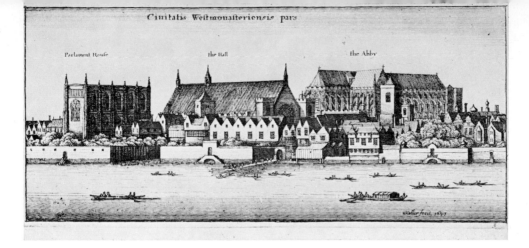

29 Although this well-known view of Westminster was drawn by Hollar in 1647 it shows a scene that had changed little since the fourteenth century. As Westminster was a royal palace and housed the courts of justice and administrative departments like the Exchequer, it formed a convenient, though for long not an invariable, place of meeting for Parliaments. St Stephen's Chapel, designated here as the Parliament House, did not become the home of the Commons until 1549. Until then the Commons usually met in the refectory of Westminster Abbey. The meeting place of the Lords lay to the left of this picture, half obscured by St Stephen's Chapel.

30 By the fourteenth century a Parliament was considered the only proper occasion for the promulgation of the most solemn acts of state. Thus in 1399 the deposition of Richard II was carried through in Parliament. This illumination from the contemporary account of Creton, who accompanied Richard on his last journey to Ireland, shows the session of 30 September. The spiritual lords are on the left, the temporal on the right. The throne is vacant. To the right, wearing a tall fur cap, stands Henry of Lancaster, ready to take his place on the throne.

31 Froissart's version of Richard II's deposition, showing him handing the emblems of sovereignty to Henry of Lancaster, is more picturesque and perhaps less exact than Creton's; but it has the merit of putting the role of Parliament in correct perspective, for the parliamentary proceedings only gave constitutional colour to an act of force. The armed men on both flanks indicate this truth. Note the kneeling clerk who records the proceedings. On this occasion special care was taken to have a full record entered on the parliament roll to avoid the ambiguities that a century earlier attended the deposition of Edward II.

32 The cultural unity of medieval Wales found expression not only in a common language but a common code of law, attributed to Hywel Dda in the tenth century. These laws remained in force in various versions until the Edwardian Conquest. Shown here is a twelfth-century Latin digest of the version current in South Wales. This section concerns officers of the royal court: three—the groom, bard and smith—are illustrated. Their functions reflect a warlike society. The bard, for example, has to sing an heroic ode to inspire the warriors and is entitled to a share of their booty.

33 Llewelyn the Great on his deathbed in 1240, after a reign of 46 years. This drawing by the contemporary English chronicler Matthew Paris shows the Prince of Wales with his sons Davydd and Gruffydd. The struggle between these brothers for the succession illustrates the family rivalries that were the bane of Welsh politics.

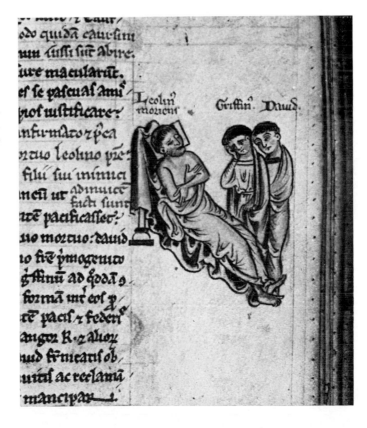

34, 35 Two castles, the contrast between which helps to explain the Edwardian conquest of Wales. *Above:* Dolwyddelan Castle, Caernarvonshire, one of the few surviving structures associated with the native princes of North Wales, traditionally birthplace of Llewelyn the Great. Built, or reconstructed, towards the end of the twelfth century, it defended the pass running through Snowdonia between Bettws-y-Coed and Ffestiniog. Note its elementary form and isolated setting, characteristic of native Welsh castles. *Below:* The castle and town of Caernarvon, brutal evidence of Edwardian power, consist of a masterpiece of medieval fortification and a planned urban settlement designed to support the castle's functions. In its original state, when the walls of the town were almost surrounded by water, bridged only by the main gateway on the left, it must have appeared a formidable, alien island of urbanism amidst the pastoral Welsh.

36 This humble building, known as St Margaret's Chapel, Edinburgh Castle, provides, in its small way, architectural evidence of the Anglo-Norman influences that contributed to the development of the Scottish monarchy. Margaret, grand-niece of Edward the Confessor, married Malcolm Canmore in 1067 and used her position as queen to introduce the Roman at the expense of Celtic rites into the Scottish Church and draw Scotland into the culture of Latin Christendom. She was canonised in 1250. The building that bears her name was probably built by one of her younger sons at the end of the twelfth century. This photograph of the interior shows characteristic Anglo-Norman influence in the chancel arch, which is heavily enriched with a deep-cut chevron pattern.

37 The Honours of Scotland and Crown Jewels, characteristic symbols of regal dignity. The elaborate Crown consists of a gold fillet, surmounted with crosses and fleurs-de-lys, closed with arches of gold wire and topped with an enamelled golden orb and cross. The whole is lavishly decorated with pearls and precious stones. The Crown was remodelled in 1540; but the jewels, arches, orb and central cross are medieval. The Sceptre was made in the fifteenth and altered in the sixteenth century. The Sword of State was presented to James IV by Pope Julius II in 1507; the sword-belt lies in front, the scabbard at the left. On the extreme right lies a rod, possibly dating from the sixteenth century, which, though known as the Lord Treasurer's mace, may have been a queen's sceptre. In the centre are jewels bequeathed to George III by the Cardinal of York, last direct descendant of the House of Stuart.

38, 39 The normanisation of Scotland, which consolidated the power of the monarchy, was distinguished, among other things, by the encouragement of the religious orders and foundation of monasteries. These communities were largely recruited from Normans and Frenchmen. The illuminated initial shown above is taken from the charter granted to Kelso Abbey by Malcolm IV in 1159. Within the initial are portraits of the young king and his grandfather David I. *Below:* Following the Anglo-Norman pattern the Scottish kings acquired a Great Seal. This example belongs to the last years before the War of Independence. It is the Great Seal of John Baliol, whose claim to the disputed succession was recognised by the arbitration of Edward I in 1292. John's reign did not last in practice beyond 1296, when he was carried off a prisoner to England. For a while, however, the Scots still recognised him; Wallace governing in his name.

40 The Palace of Holyrood House. Its construction in the late fifteenth century followed the recognition of Edinburgh as the chief town in Scotland and the adoption of more sedentary administrative habits. Though just outside the town gates it stood within safe distance of Edinburgh Castle, so often the refuge of Scottish rulers. The architecture of the James IV tower, on the left, all that survives of the original palace, reflects the insecurity of the age and continental, perhaps French, influences. The rest of the building, including the tower on the right, belongs to the reconstruction made by Robert Mylne on the orders of Charles II.

41 Even more than Holyroodhouse the palace block at Stirling Castle shows how thoroughly by the end of the Middle Ages Scotland had rejected English influences. James V, who had this built in 1540, spent some time at the French court and married a daughter of Francis I; and the French alliance seems clearly reflected in the Renaissance decoration with its statues, wall shafts and foliage.

42 The interior of the Scottish Parliament Hall, empty since the Union, with nothing to distinguish it but its splendid roof. It was only after 1587, when the shire members began to attend, that the Parliament, hitherto infrequent and mostly content with the Edinburgh Tolbooth, required accommodation appropriate to its size and status; and it was not until 1632 that the citizens, pressed by Charles I and anxious to keep the sessions in their town, built the present Parliament House with the help of private subscribers. Only one hall was required as the three estates met together.

43 Borthwick Castle, Midlothian, built by Sir William, later Lord, Borthwick in 1430, an outstanding example of the tower-houses made necessary by the insecurity of this period. Although exceptionally grand, it presents the austere aspect of a place of refuge, with walls twelve to fourteen feet thick below and windows as small and few as possible. The main entrance was on the first floor, approached not, as in less elaborate towers, by an easily-removed ladder but by a bridge from the curtain wall. The wide-mouthed gun-ports were inserted in the curtain wall in the sixteenth century. Houses of this type continued to be built in Scotland in the sixteenth and seventeenth centuries.

44 Cockle Park Tower, near Morpeth, Northumberland, built in the early sixteenth century, one of the numerous Pele Towers occasioned by the insecurity of the North. It has two rounded turrets at its northern end. The battlement of one of them projects on the right; and, by it, surmounted by a gable, is a projection containing a spiral staircase. Such houses, offering protection against native raiders as much as against the Scots, remained necessary until at least the seventeenth century.

45 In the South the old order passed away more quickly. Cowdray House in Sussex illustrates its passing, for it is said to be the last building in England for which a licence to crenellate was issued, in 1533. This view of the western entrance gatehouse, built by the 1st Earl of Southampton, suggests that the crenellations were valued more for ornament than defence. Dr Johnson, who visited the house not long before it was destroyed by fire, said of it: 'Sir, I should like to stay here four-and-twenty hours. We see here how our ancestors lived.'

46, 47
48, 49 The majesty of the Tudor monarchy and the supremacy of King-in-Parliament: a contemporary picture, *above left*, of the opening of Parliament in 1523. The ceremony reveals the stages of Parliament's development. The king, counsellors and judges form the visible core. Henry VIII sits in isolated splendour. On his right hand sits the Chancellor, Wolsey, beneath the device of a cardinal's hat. In the centre, seated on woolsacks, are the judges, masters in chancery and other counsellors summoned by special writ. The next component consists of the lords, the spiritual outnumbering the temporal peers. Other peers sit on a cross bench: on their right is the Prior of St John of Jerusalem. The Commons, standing at the bar of the House, their Speaker in the middle, form the last component; their position is a relic of their former inessential status. Note the clerks behind the lower woolsack keeping a record of the proceedings. *Above right:* This title page of Cranmer's Bible in English illustrates a revolution, the establishment of royal supremacy over the church. At the top Henry VIII communicates with God without Papal intercession. Below God, the king, as spiritual head, hands bibles to Archbishop Cranmer and Thomas Cromwell, who distribute them to laymen as well as clergy. The people give thanks. The blank circle (right centre) bore, in the first edition, the arms of Cromwell. When this second edition was published in 1541 the all-powerful minister had been executed and so his arms were expunged. *Opposite above:* The Gatehouse of St Albans Abbey, built in 1365, served as courthouse and gaol for the Liberty or jurisdiction enjoyed by the Abbot over almost the whole hundred in which the Abbey and borough lay. The Abbot's rights enabled him to appoint his own justices of the peace and control the borough. This supremacy had caused friction; but it was not until the Reformation that the laity were emancipated from their ecclesiastical lords. The Liberty of St Albans then fell into the king's hands. The Gatehouse came under new management but continued to serve as sessions house and gaol. The borough, released from its dependence, had its new status recognised by a royal charter; and its mayor replaced the Abbot's bailiff. *Opposite below:* The Royal Arms in the church of Tivetshall St Margaret, Norfolk, are a splendid rare example, being those of Elizabeth I. Replacing the rood, they proclaimed the Royal Supremacy re-established in 1559.

50, 51 The Reformation had its victims on both sides. The Carthusians, *above*, unlike most monks, did not tamely accept the new order; and this engraving of 1555 depicts their martyrdom. They suffered the penalties of treason, not heresy; for they rejected the Royal Supremacy. The scenes show them being dragged to Tyburn, hanged, drawn, and quartered, and their limbs being boiled before decorating the walls of London. In Mary's reign came the turn of Protestant martyrs. Latimer and Ridley, *below*, are about to be burned at the stake outside the walls of Oxford in 1555. Lord Williams of Thame, presiding, holds up the warrant of execution. From a pulpit the Regius Professor of Divinity delivers a sermon, while Cranmer looks down from the Bocardo prison: he was burned a year later. Burning remained the punishment for heresy until the early seventeenth century.

A briefe note of the benefits that grow to this Realme,

by the observation of Fish-daies: with a reason and cause wherefore the lawe in that behalfe made, is ordained. Very necessary to be placed in the houses of all men, specially common Victualers.

Here heretofore by the Queenes most excellent Maiestie, of her clemencie and rare conceiued, for diuers priuate benefits that might growe to her louing subiects, specially for the better maintenance of the Nauie of this lande, hath with the assent of the whole state of her Realme, caused to be made & pub-

52 Concern for the navy led Elizabeth I to compel observance of 'fish days', prohibiting meat on Fridays or during Lent—and sometimes on Wednesdays also. This continued medieval practice, but with a difference. This abstinence had a political purpose and the government made it an offence to suggest otherwise. However, its papistical associations reinforced people's natural reluctance to obey. Hence the necessity of pamphlets like this to advocate the merits of the 'Protestant Lent'. Non-observance incurred severe penalties; but the wealthy could buy exemption.

53 Part of a sumptuary proclamation by which Elizabeth I tried to restrict her subjects to the dress appropriate to their social rank. In the preamble she complains of the 'confusion of degrees' that follows when 'the meanest are as richly apparalled as their betters' and of the waste of national resources entailed by the spirit of emulation in dress. She lays down detailed rules, a summary of which is illustrated here, to regulate the materials that might be used by the various ranks of society. Sumptuary regulations were not new, but Elizabeth's attempt to enforce them illustrates her concern to maintain the social hierarchy and to protect the national economy. There is no evidence that the proclamation had any effect.

Imprinted at London by the Deputies of
Christopher Barker, printer to the Queenes
most excellent Maiestie.

1597.

54 Edward III weights, Winchester. To promote the wool trade and his revenue, Edward III standardised the avoirdupois pound. Standard measures were kept in the Exchequer and equivalent sets sent out to the towns. Winchester received the five smaller weights, ranging from 7 to 56 lbs, in 1340 and the large 'quarter woolsack' of 91 lbs in 1387. They are bronze, with iron rings. They bear the royal cypher on top and the Plantagenet arms round the body. This successful operation illustrates the power and unity of the medieval state.

55 The great recoinage carried through between 1560 and 1561 was one of the most creditable and successful of Tudor achievements. In the middle of the century the coinage had been gravely debased: Elizabeth now restored the old 'sterling' standard first established in Anglo-Saxon times. In the past coining was done by provincial mints which were supplied with dies made in London. The consolidation of the country and improvement in communications made it possible to dispense with these by Edward VI's reign and Elizabeth's operation was carried out from London. At that time the Royal Mint was in the Tower. This woodcut from Holinshed's *Chronicle* shows coiners at work. On the right two men are striking coins, forcing the impression of the die on the metal by the blows of their hammers. Behind, the blanks are heated in a furnace. In front, coins are being smoothed and weighed.

56, 56a Henry VII bronze gallon of 1497, Winchester. Henry VII introduced new standards in 1497, among them for the first time a standard for the gallon, of which some 49 certified copies were sent out to the towns. The gallon shown here is inscribed in relief with the king's name. On the rim are three verification marks consisting of a crown over a Roman 'E': these were stamped on when the measure was checked by the Exchequer in the reign of Elizabeth I. It still agrees exactly with the Exchequer Standard Gallon of 1497 now preserved at the Science Museum, South Kensington: it has a capacity of 155 fl. ounces. *Below:* Henry VII yard, Winchester. The yard—for measuring cloth—had long been standardised when this was issued in about 1497. It is a hexagonal bar of bronze: at one end it is sealed with a bronze cap with a Lombardic 'h' for Henry VII, at the other with an iron cap with an 'E' for Elizabeth, probably added when it was adjusted in her reign. The smaller divisions show $18''$, $9''$, $4\frac{1}{2}''$, $2\frac{1}{4}''$ (the 'nail') and $1\frac{1}{8}''$. Its length is that of the Imperial Standard yard less $0.0004''$.

57 The Oracle, Reading, was an unusually elaborate workhouse for the poor. This is explained by the fact that the funds were not, in the first place, provided by a rate but by a private benefaction. In 1624, John Kendrick, a clothier, left £7,500 to the corporation to build a workhouse for the poor of his native town and to purchase materials to employ them in the clothing trade. It continued in use, with some vagaries of fortune, until the early nineteenth century. Its name is difficult to account for: it has been surmised that the grand portico shown in this engraving was called an oriel and that Oriel was in time corrupted to Oracle.

58 The racking of Cuthbert Simson in Mary's reign, from a contemporary woodcut. The use of torture illustrates the power of the Tudor privy council. It exercised the discretion to use extraordinary methods and was not bound by common law, which did not recognise torture because it did not need a confession to arrive at a verdict. On this occasion the rack was used to make a Protestant reveal his fellows. It was frequently used on Catholic priests in Elizabeth's reign. Torture ceased after 1640.

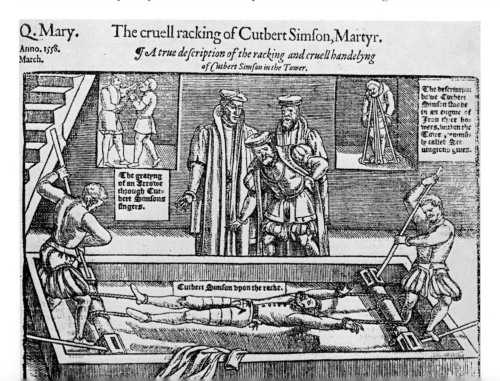

59 Star Chamber came into being to secure respect for the law. It was also its business to enforce royal proclamations; and through this function it undertook the regulation of printing. This ordinance, issued in 1586, arose out of a case involving a breach of an earlier proclamation about printing. In deciding this case Star Chamber took the opportunity to lay down definitive rules about censorship.

60 The King's Manor, York, provides the most evident visual relic of the Council of the North. Although the Council was originally intended to be peripatetic, it established itself in 1538 in York on the site of the suppressed abbey of St Mary's. From that time successive Presidents added to the buildings, creating an ensemble that testified to the grandeur of the Council. This picture shows part of the additions made by Thomas Wentworth, Earl of Strafford, last and greatest of Presidents. Note his arms set above the door. This was charged against him as an act of arrogance when he was impeached in 1640.

61, 62 *Above:* The Sidney monument in the chancel of St Laurence's church, Ludlow, conveys something of the dignity attached to the office of Lord President of the Council of the Marches. Sir Henry Sidney held the office from 1559 until his death in 1586, though much of the time he was employed in Ireland and acted at Ludlow through a deputy. The monument commemorates his daughter Ambrosia, sister of Sir Philip Sidney. *Above right:* This engraving of the Seal of the Council of the Marches makes a point that renders this council unique among the conciliar courts: at the Restoration it was revived and functioned, though obscurely, until 1689. Its civil jurisdiction had always been valued and its reputation had not been so deeply blackened by political activities as that of the Council of the North. However, it was too closely associated with royal absolutism to survive the Glorious Revolution.

63 Ludlow Castle, *right*, was an important seat of
government long before it housed the Council of
the Marches. In the fourteenth century it was the
administrative headquarters of the extensive
marcher lordships acquired by the Mortimers.
In the next century these estates passed to the
house of York; and Ludlow became one of the
bastions of Yorkist power during the Wars of the
Roses. When Edward IV became king the council
which had administered his marcher estates from
Ludlow became a royal council and developed insensibly into an administration for the whole of
Wales and the Marches.

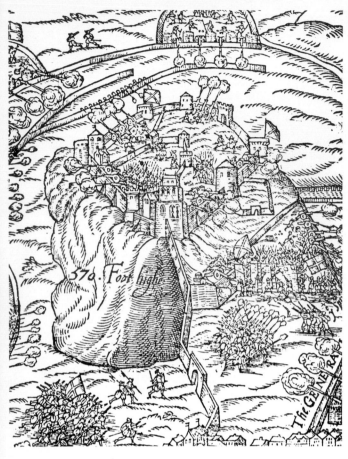

64 The Siege of Edinburgh, 1573. Holinshed's animated sketch brings to life an important episode in Anglo-Scottish relations, when Elizabeth I sent a small force to help the Scottish Protestants eject the partisans of Mary Queen of Scots from Edinburgh Castle. This made possible the triumph of the reformers, the eventual union of the crowns and pacification of the Border.

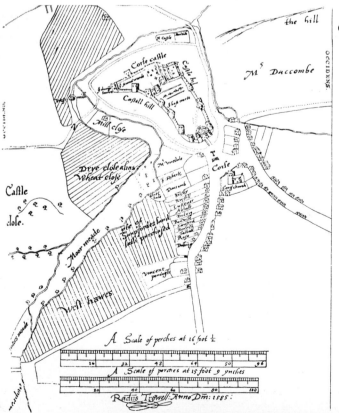

65 Corfe in 1586. The gallows (top left), stocks and pillory (between the castle and the church) testify to the jurisdiction the lord of Corfe still retained in Tudor times. Although long a borough by prescription and incorporated by royal charter in 1576, Corfe remained dependent on the castle. Its lord's jurisdiction covered the whole Isle of Purbeck. As hereditary lord lieutenant, admiral, and governor of the forest, he appointed all officers, mustered the militia and held the courts. No islander might marry out of the island or erect a house, without his licence.

66, 67 The development of the office of Justice of the Peace gradually undermined other local jurisdictions. In Elizabeth's reign its importance created a demand for manuals of instruction, made necessary because the justices were mostly laymen, not learned in the law. *Eirenarcha* was the most successful of these manuals. It was reprinted seven times between 1582 and 1610 and remained a standard authority until the end of the eighteenth century. This edition contains as appendix a table of the statutes which concerned the justices of the peace. It lists 298 statutes, of which 169 dated from the Tudor period. *Below:* Much Wenlock Guildhall has provided the court room of the justices since 1577, when this upper storey was added to a medieval base. Over the chairman's seat is a Latin inscription to the effect that: 'This place abhors iniquity, loves peace, punishes wrongdoing, upholds the law, honours the upright.' The room contains wheeled stocks, last used in 1852. From 1468 until 1885 the borough returned two members to parliament. After 1679 one of them was always—except for an interval of 15 years—from the Forester family.

EIRENARCHA: or of *The office of the Iustices* of Peace in foure Bookes.

Gathered 1579: first published 1581: and now secondly reuised, corrected, and enlarged agreeably to the reformed Commission of the Peace, in this 34. yeare of the peaceable raigne of our most gratious Queene ELIZABETH.

By WILLIAM LAMBARD of Lincolnes Inne, Gent.

Ha tibi erunt artes, pacique imponere morem.

AT LONDON,
Printed by Ralph Newbery.
Cum Priuilegio.

Anno Domini, 1592.

68, The title-page of Coke's *Reports*, published between
69 1600 and 1616. These comprehensive accounts of
contemporary cases exemplify the revival of
Common Law jurisprudence. They were immediately accepted as authoritative and remained so for
two hundred years, being last reprinted in 1826.
They formed a companion work to Coke's *In-
stitutes*, which were an exposition of the principles
of the law. The title-page, like the *Reports* themselves, is written in the Norman-French that the
courts used until the eighteenth century. *Below:*
Westminster Hall, an early Stuart drawing of the
south end, showing the Courts of King's Bench
(*left*) and Chancery (*right*). The Hall, 250 feet long,
70 feet across, built by William II, was still the
largest in England. The Court of Common Pleas
was held midway along the west wall and the Court
of Exchequer in a room adjoining the north-west
corner. Steps near the King's Bench led directly
to the Commons' lobby: this proximity facilitated
the relationship between law and politics. The
Hall had inconveniences, being notoriously noisy,
thronged with lawyers, clients and the general
public, housing bookstalls and other shops. In
1820 the courts were removed to adjacent rooms
and in 1882 to Street's building in the Strand.

70 The cult of monarchy was a marked feature of Tudor government. Here is a popular example of the cult, in the form of a woodcut portrait of Elizabeth I, decked in the most elaborate and regal finery, with adulatory verses by Giles Godhead printed beneath. This was published in 1563.

71 The presentation of the Speaker in the Parliament of 1584. The first act of the Commons after the State Opening was to choose their Speaker, nomination in practice being made by the Privy Council. A few days later they presented him to the Queen. Summoned to the bar, they led in the Speaker Elect between two Privy Councillors. After a conventional 'disabling' speech of self-deprecation he was confirmed by the Queen and then made the traditional petition for the privileges of the House. This granted, parliamentary business could begin. Note how lay peers now outnumber spiritual peers and the monarch's dignity is enhanced by greater isolation; but ceremony has not kept pace with the importance of the Commons, who remain behind the bar.

72 The House of Commons in 1624, probably the earliest picture of the House; and its publication indicates how the importance of the Commons was publicly recognised. The House is shown meeting in St Stephen's Chapel, their permanent home from 1549 until 1834. The seating plan of the Chapel, which divided members into opposing rows, still distinguishes the English parliamentary pattern. It was already customary for privy councillors to occupy what is now the government front bench. The chapel was even then too small to seat all members after the Tudor expansion. The engraving shows the Commons exercising their right to discipline those who infringed their privileges. The offender, in custody of the Serjeant-at-Arms, kneels at the bar waiting sentence.

73 This woodcut from a contemporary broadside expresses the unpopularity of the financial expedients to which the early Stuarts resorted. This shows Sir Giles Mompesson, most notorious of the courtiers and politicians who profited from these devices, engaged in enforcing the patent granted him to license alehouses. Having paid well for the patent he recouped himself by charging exorbitant fees and exacting heavy fines. In 1621 the Commons investigated the licensing patent. Mompesson was sentenced to imprisonment for life and a fine of £10,000.

74 This proclamation of 1633 for the regulation of prices illustrates the revival of conciliar activity and royal paternalism that marked the 'personal' government of Charles I.

By the King.

A Proclamation for the prizes of Poultry,
Rabbits, Butter, Candles, Charcoale, and all manner of Fuell of Wood.

Here of late by seuerall Inquisitions taken before *Charles Walker*, Gentleman, Deputy to Hugh Maye Esquire Clarke of the Market of Our houshold, and throughout Our Kingdome of England, in Our City of Westminster and elsewhere, in Our County of Middlesex, and in Our Borough of Southwarke, in Our County of Surry, which was done in the presence and with the aduice of diuers of Our Justices of the Peace of Our said Counties and City, wee then in Our Royall person being at Our Court of White-Hall, it was found and presented by the oathes of three Enquests of twelue lawfull men of the said Counties and City, seuerally sworne (to enquire of the prizes of seuerall things in the said Inquisitions mentioned) that the prizes after mentioned are reasonable prizes to bee obserued by Poulterers, Uictualers, Woodmongers, and all others within three miles of any of the Gates of Our City of London, for the seuerall sorts of Uictualls and other things after specified. That is to say;

A fat Cignet of the best sort vntill Alhallontide	vij. s.
The like Cignet from Alhallontide to Lent	ix. s.
The best Phesant Cocke	vj. s.
A Phesant Henne	v. s.
A Phesant Pout	iij. s. iiij. d.
A Turkey-Cocke, the best in the market	iiij. s. iiij. d.
The like best Turkey-Cocke at the Poulterers Shop	iiij. s. vj. d.
The best Turkey-Henne in the market	iij. s.

75 The distrust aroused by the Stuarts was stimulated above all by fear of their religious and foreign policies. They were suspected of being too favourable to the Spaniards and papists, who were thought to be plotting to overthrow the religion and liberties of Protestant Europe. When Prince Charles went in person to Madrid in 1623 to negotiate marriage with the Princess Maria of Spain, hysterical fears were excited at home for his and the country's fate. Intense relief was expressed when he returned, unmarried and still a Protestant. This woodcut shows the prince kneeling before his father while the people rejoice.

76 During the 'eleven years' tyranny' Star Chamber, hitherto a popular court, acquired a bad reputation for its part in silencing the critics of the regime and of the bishops in particular. One of the most outspoken critics was John Lilburne, who was accused in 1637 of circulating libels against the bishops. Refusing to plead before the court, he was sentenced to be whipped from the Fleet prison to Westminster, to stand in the pillory and to be kept in prison until he should change his mind. This contemporary Dutch picture shows Lilburne being whipped through the streets. The penalty was regarded as particularly arbitrary because corporal punishment was considered degrading and usually reserved for the lower orders.

77 This crude woodcut, taken from a broadside entitled *A Looking Glass for Statesmen*, shows the execution of the two chief agents of the 'eleven years' tyranny', Laud and Strafford. Strafford was executed in 1641, Laud in 1645. This was an age which delighted in scriptural parallels and so they are compared with false statesmen like Haman, Saul and Achitophel. The broadside says of Strafford that he 'wanted nothing to secure greatness but goodness'.

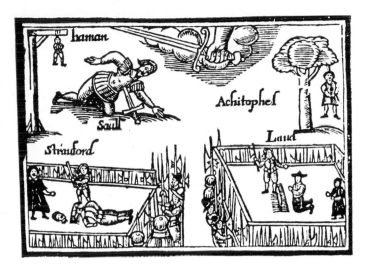

78 Charles I hoped to achieve a reconciliation with the Long Parliament by sacrificing Strafford and abandoning conciliar methods of government. But hopes of a peaceful constitutional settlement were destroyed by his attempt at a *coup d'état* in January 1642 when he tried to seize the leaders of the opposition. This drawing by Hollar shows the king entering the Commons with a body of armed men in defiance of the privileges of the House; but the five members had been warned and took refuge in the City. After this the majority of the Commons could no longer trust the king to respect the law; and Charles, aware of his blunder, left London, never to return until his execution.

79 Charles I's instructions, in his own hand, for the impeachment of the Five Members. Before the king attempted to arrest the opposition leaders he had already prepared their impeachment before the Lords, charging them with attempting to 'subvert the fundamental laws and government of the kingdom of England, to deprive the King of his regal power, and to place in subjects an arbitrary and tyrannical power over the lives, liberties and estates of His Majesty's liege people'. The plan was to ask the peers to appoint a secret committee to examine the evidence; and since it was important to prevent the leading opposition peers, named here, from being elected to the committee, their nomination was to be opposed on the excuse mentioned. Lord Mandeville's name, which originally appeared on this list, was scratched off, as it was later decided to impeach him as well as the commoners; hence the alteration made to the number of the accused. In all this the king was preparing to act legally. But the accusation of a peer offended the Lords, who delayed action; and the Commons, encouraged, refused to allow their accused members to be arrested in the ordinary way by the Serjeant-at-Arms. It was this check to his plans that led the king to abandon strictly legal means and attempt to make the arrest by force.

80 The Civil War was accompanied by a battle in the press. This title-page belongs to a royalist contribution to the debate. Dudley Digges, who was a young Fellow of All Souls, maintained the extreme thesis that subjects had no right to resist their king on any pretext, but added, as a concession to weaker brethren, that in this case the king was also fighting on the side of law and the constitution against the revolutionary demands of parliament. Note the medallion below, showing the armed figure of rebellion trampling the crown underfoot and shaking hands with a witch.

THE
Unlawfulneſs
OF
SUBJECTS
Takeing up Armes
against their
SOVERAIGNE
in what Caſe ſoever
Written by
Dudley Diggs G.
late Fellow of All-Soules
Colledge in Oxford

81 The execution of Charles I, 30 January 1649. This painting by an unknown foreign artist, possibly Weesop, shows how this was conducted in the most public and solemn manner. The regicides believed that they were inflicting a just sentence on a criminal king, convicted after a legal trial.

82 Charles I dead aided the royalist cause more than Charles I alive. The image of the monarch could no longer be soiled by the deeds of the man; and the cult of Charles the Martyr followed rapidly on his execution. In 1649 there was published the *Eikon Basilike*, one of the most successful pamphlets ever written, which went rapidly into 47 editions. Written probably by John Gauden, it purported to represent the reflections of the king himself, composed during his captivity. It justified him as a martyr for the constitution and the church. The emblematic frontispiece reproduced here conveys with studied symbolism the concept of the Royal Martyr: the king's virtues increase even under the weight of his miseries; he stands like a rock, unmoved by storms; he spurns the empty splendour of his earthly crown and, taking the thorny crown of martyrdom, looks up to a heavenly crown of glory.

83 Monarchy is hydra-headed. Charles II succeeded to the claims of his father. The Scottish Presbyterians, who feared the religious extremism of the English regicides, refused to recognise the new republic and in 1651 crowned Charles II at Scone. This woodcut shows his coronation, after he had promised to respect the church and constitution.

A Speech made by K. Charles y. 2ᵈ at his Coronation: 1 January: 1651

I will by gods assistance bestow my life for your defence wishing to live no longer then that I may see this Kingdome flourish in happiness .

The Oath, I doe promise & vow in y presence of y eternall god y I will maintaine y true Kirk of god religion right preaching & administration of y Sacraments now received & preached within this Realme in purity; And shall abolish & gain-stand all false Religions & sects contrary to y same. And shall rule y people comitted to my charge according to y will of god, and laudable laws & constitutions of y Realme; causing justice & equity to be ministred without partiality

84 The Great Seal of the Commonwealth, showing the Rump or purged Long Parliament in session. Note the inscription; there is an ironic contrast between the oligarchic character of the Rump and its claim to have established an era of liberty.

85 A Dutch satire on the dissolution of the Rump, 20 April 1653. Cromwell watches in the foreground while his troopers eject the Speaker from the chair and hustle the members from the House. The breach between the Army and the Rump marked the first serious division in the republican ranks. The dissolution left the Army in power but deprived it of any constitutional basis for its authority.

86 This Restoration satire portrays *The Commonwealth ruleing with a standing Army*. The Commonwealth is a dragon which devours the people's traditional laws, liberties and institutions and their 'gaine' or wealth. As its fruits it excretes taxes, excise and other burdens that are imposed on the people, while its dupes, their liberties turned to chains, cry 'O wonderful Reformation'.

87 A favourable interpretation of the Interregnum. William Fairthorne's elaborate allegory depicts Cromwell as Protector, master of the three kingdoms, restoring order after the flood of anarchy, trampling on iniquity, while countrymen pursue their rustic tasks and a helmet is put to peaceful use as a hive for bees. Even so, plotters conspire against the pillar of the state.

The Army Entring
the City ~

The Rump & dreggs of y̌ house o
Commons Sitting after y̌ Army
had turnd y̌ good members o̱

...iver seeking God whil
̌he King is murthered
by his order ~

Bradshaw the Taylor,
and y̌ Hangman keeper
of the Liberty̌es of England

88 A royalist version of events leading to the Restoration. Although these plates are taken from a Tory pamphlet of 1683, the original prints were probably made between 1659 and 1660 for the Cavalier exiles in Holland. Their purpose is to show the republican regimes as arbitrary and tyrannical, and the restoration of monarchy as the guarantee of freedom. The story begins with the Army's march on London in 1647, its first intervention in politics and the first act of arbitrary power. Later the king's execution is welcomed by a mounted Jesuit, who regards him as the worst enemy of the papists. After the king's death Bradshaw is singled out because he was President of the Rump's council of state and also presided at the trial of the king and a number of royalist leaders.

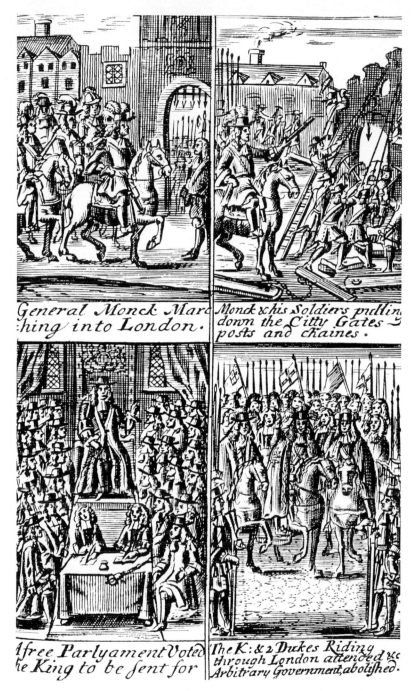

General Monck Marc

hing into London.

Monck & his Soldiers pulling

down the Citty Gates &

posts and chaines.

A free Parlyament Voted

he King to be sent for

The K: & 2 Dukes Riding

through London attended &c

Arbitrary Government, abolished.

89 A continuation of the same. In 1659, after the Protectorate had collapsed on Cromwell's death, the Army's leaders recalled the Rump. But Army and Rump quarrelled again, the military commanders quarrelled among themselves, the City of London defied them all and demanded the restoration of the old Long Parliament. Early in 1660 General Monck, whom Cromwell had put in command of the Scottish garrisons and who now controlled the only reliable troops, marched south, ostensibly to secure the authority of the Rump. His troops are shown entering the City on the Rump's orders and destroying its defences. This was followed by a *volte-face* which transformed the situation. Once in the City Monck adopted its cause. The Rump was forced to admit the members excluded in 1648 and the restored Long Parliament at once ordered free elections. The sequel is clear.

90 The Coronation of Charles II in Westminster Abbey, 1661. New regalia had to be made for the occasion, the old having been destroyed in the Interregnum. The new crown, however, like the old, was known as St Edward's crown and so preserved at least in name the connection with the Anglo-Saxon monarchy. This etching by Hollar shows two stages of the ceremony, the Crowning and the Presentation.

91 The Coronation Procession of Charles II. The Procession from the Tower to Westminster was an integral part of the ancient coronation ceremonies. It was therefore revived in 1661. It took place the day before the actual coronation. Pepys, who watched it, records that 'it is impossible to relate the glory of this day'.

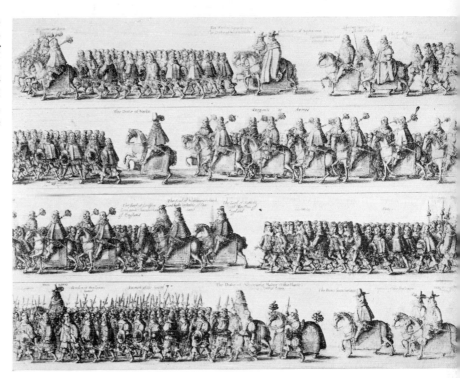

92 Because the Restoration was not brought about by the victory of any one party it was not accompanied by much bloodshed. But fifty-seven persons, mostly regicides or closely connected with them, were excepted from the Act of Indemnity passed by the Convention Parliament. Eleven of them were executed by the barbarous procedure reserved for traitors since the reign of Edward I. This contemporary print shows them being hanged and quartered. Pepys afterwards saw some of their limbs exposed on Aldersgate.

A representation of the execution of the Kings Judges.

The Popes Cheife Agent was soe poor
He Begd an Almes at Pickerins dore.

Describe Don John.

A tall black man

Since naught but blowes is to be got
Wise Oates discovers Iesuits Plot.

93 Titus Oates before the Council during the Popish Plot in 1678. This plausible adventurer revealed a conspiracy to kill Charles II, put his brother on the throne and restore Catholicism. Though trapped by the king into a false description of Don John of Austria, whom he claimed to have met, Oates was believed by the Council. Fear of popery reached hysterical proportions and the Plot dominated politics for over two years, nearly leading to a change in the succession and civil war.

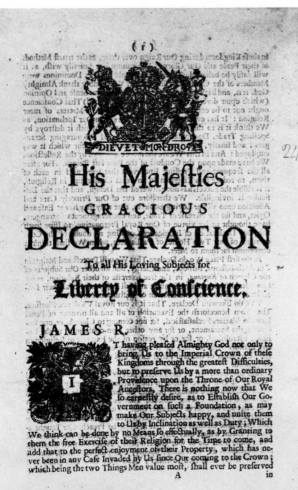

(1)

DIEV·ET·MON·DROIT

His Majesties
GRACIOUS
DECLARATION
To all His Loving Subjects for
Liberty of Conscience.

JAMES R.

I

T having pleased Almighty God not only to bring Us to the Imperial Crown of these Kingdoms through the greatest Difficulties, but to preserve Us by a more than ordinary Providence upon the Throne of Our Royal Ancestors, There is nothing now that We so earnestly desire, as to Establish Our Government on such a Foundation, as may make Our Subjects happy, and unite them to Us by Inclination as well as Duty; Which We think can be done by no Means so effectually, as by Granting to them the free Exercise of their Religion for the Time to come, and add that to the perfect enjoyment of their Property, which has never been in any Case Invaded by Us since Our coming to the Crown; which being the two Things Men value most, shall ever be preserved

A   in

94 The Whigs, who had hoped to use the Popish Plot to exclude James, Duke of York, from the throne, had been thwarted; and in 1685 he became king with the support of a strong Tory reaction. Yet within three years he had driven Whigs and Tories together into a national opposition. The Declaration of Indulgence, shown here, provides part of the explanation. Its offer of toleration to Roman Catholic as well as Protestant dissenters seemed not only an unconstitutional act of royal prerogative but an infringement of the privileged status of the Anglican Church. When the king issued a second Declaration in 1688 and ordered the clergy to read it from their pulpits he provoked a public protest from the bishops. His attempt to coerce the Church by putting the bishops on trial did more than any other single act to bring about the Glorious Revolution.

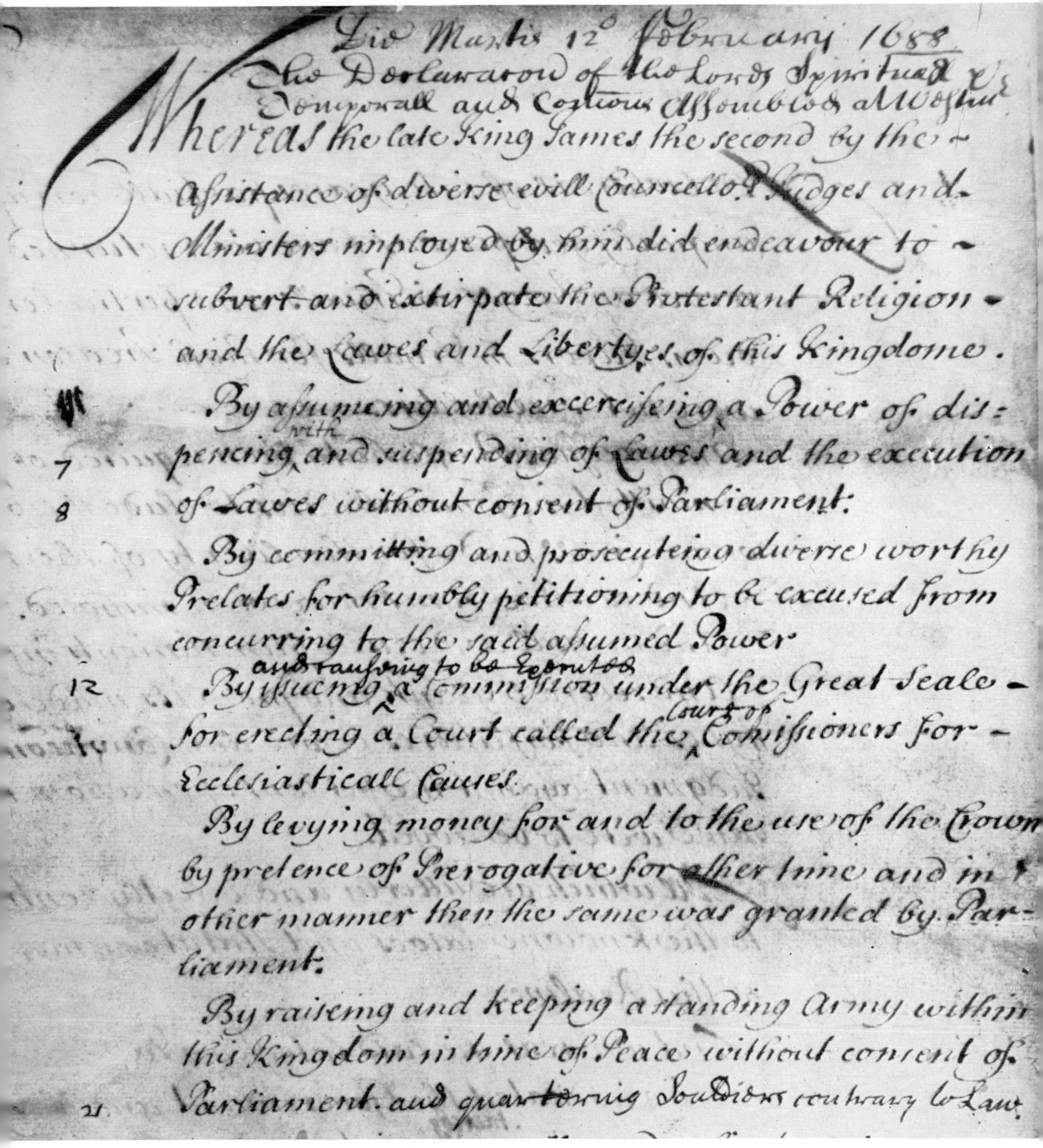

Die Martis 12° February 1688

The Declaration of the Lords Spirituall &
Temporall and Comons Assembled at Westm'r

Whereas the late King James the second by the
assistance of diverse evill Councellors Judges and
Ministers imployed by him did endeavour to
subvert and extirpate the Protestant Religion
and the Lawes and Libertyes of this Kingdome.

By assumeing and excerceiseing a Power of dis:
pencing ^with and suspending of Lawes and the execution
of Lawes without consent of Parliament:

By committing and prosecuteing diverse worthy
Prelates for humbly petitioning to be excused from
concurring to the said assumed Power

By issueing ~~and causeing to be executed~~ ^a Commission under the Great Seale
for erecting a Court called the ^Court of Comissioners for
Ecclesiasticall Causes.

By levying money for and to the use of the Crown
by pretence of Prerogative for other time and in
other manner then the same was granted by Parliament.

By raiseing and keeping a standing Army within
this Kingdom in time of Peace without consent of
Parliament. and quartering Souldiers contrary to Law.

7
8

12

21

95 The Declaration of Rights, 12 February 1689. This shows the beginning of the original Declaration
drafted by the Commons and amended by the Lords. It was only after accepting this Declaration that
William and Mary became king and queen.

96 The Coronation of William and Mary, 11 April 1689. Note their equality of status. They kneel on the same level, have similar crowns and sceptres, and two orbs are ready to be handed to them. The ceremony was performed by the Bishop of London, as Archbishop Sancroft, though one of the Seven Bishops put on trial by James II, had scruples about breaking his oath of allegiance to the late king.

97 The Act of Union of the two Kingdoms of England and Scotland being presented to Queen Anne by the Duke of Queensberry, 1707. As the royal commissioner to the Scottish parliament Queensberry had most responsibility for negotiating the completion of the treaty. This earned him a lasting unpopularity among his fellow-countrymen, but also some compensation in the form of the title of Duke of Dover and a pension of £3,000. Note the new Union flag. Article 1 of the Act provided that 'the crosses of St George and St Andrew be conjoined in such manner as her Majesty shall think fit, and used in all flags, banners, standards and ensigns both at sea and land'.

98 The Militia Bill of 1708, the last occasion on which the royal veto was used. Note (top left) the traditional Norman-French formula in which the Queen's refusal is conveyed.

Ludwig Scandford.   *Soit Baille aux Seigneurs*

Cheste Bille les seigneurs
sont Assentus

Whereas the Militia of the severall parts of the United Kingdom of Great Britain were before the Union established in a different manner and it will be for the Strengthning and perfecting of the Happy Union that the Militia of the whole united Kingdom should be put on the same Establishment and Regulation **Be it therefore Enacted by**

THE ROYALL HO... ...ELSEY

99, 100 Chelsea Hospital for invalid soldiers reminds us of the growth of the professional standing army. The hospital was conceived by Charles II after the example of the *Invalides* at Paris, designed by Wren and opened in 1692. Mary II emulated this humanitarian benefaction by founding the hospital for sailors at Greenwich. *Above:* The exterior of Chelsea Hospital as it appeared in Wren's time. *Below:* The interior of the hall early in this century.

101, By the eighteenth century the House of Commons was securely established as the centre of political
102, power. Here are three 'Great Commoners' who rose to office through the House of Commons. *Above*
103 *left:* Sir Robert Walpole standing and addressing a meeting of councillors, about 1740. This has sometimes been taken as a meeting of the cabinet but is more likely to represent the Lords Justices appointed from time to time to form a regency council when the king was absent in Hanover. Joseph
Goupy, who painted this watercolour, was in the service of Frederick Prince of Wales. Frederick
thought that he ought to be regent himself in his father's absence and Goupy may have been instructed
in this painting to discredit the council as a body of puppets dominated by the commanding presence
of the chief minister. *Below:* J. S. Copley's painting of the fatal illness of William Pitt, Earl of Chatham,
in the House of Lords in 1778. Although Chatham died a peer, he had made his great reputation in
the Commons. His acceptance of a peerage in 1766 was highly unpopular and his subsequent political
career something of an anticlimax. Note the meticulous detail with which Copley portrayed the peers,
most of whom can be identified. *Above right:* K. A. Hickel's painting of the younger Pitt addressing
the Commons in 1793 shows the appearance of the House in the great age of parliamentary oratory.
Note that since the Union and the addition of the Scottish members further accommodation had
been supplied by the provision of galleries.

Kentish Election. 1734

The *Leicestershire* POLL,

As the same was Taken at the County-Court, holden at the Castle of *Leicester*, on *Thursday* the seventeenth Day of *December*, 1719. upon a Writt for the Electing a Knight in Parliament for the County of *Leicester* aforesaid, in the Room of Sir *Thomas Cave*, Bart. deceas'd,

Alphabetically digested.

The OATH of a Freeholder.

YOU shall Swear, That you are a Freeholder in the County of   and have Freehold Lands or Hereditaments lying or being at   in the County of   of the Yearly Value of Forty Shillings above all Charges payable out of the same ; and that such Freehold Estate hath not been Made or Granted to you Fraudulently, on purpose to Qualify you to give your Vote ; and that the Place of your Abode is at   in   and that you have not been Polled before at this Election.

London Printed : And are to be Sold by *Simon Marten,* Bookseller, at his Shops in *Leicester, Loughborough,* and *Hinck'ey,* 1720.

POLL BOOK
FOR THE
SOUTHERN DIVISION
OF
LEICESTERSHIRE.

BAGWORTH POLLING DISTRICT.

Note.—The unpolled Voters are entered at the end of the Parish for which the qualification is situate, but they may have polled for a qualification in another Parish.

PARISH OR TOWNSHIP OF BAGWORTH.

NAME:	RESIDENCE.	CURZON	PELL	PAGET
Adams, Rev. Samuel	Thornton	—	—	
Annis, Robert	Bagworth	—	—	
Bott, John	Bagworth	—	—	
Clarke, Robert	Bagworth	—	—	
Croshaw, George	Bagworth	—	—	
Crosher, James	Bagworth			—
Geary, John	Bagworth	—	—	
Dowell, Thomas	Bagworth	—	—	
Harris, Joseph Croshaw	Bagworth			
Harrison, Robert	Bagworth park	—	—	
Johnson, Joseph	Bagworth			—
Lees, John Bretnell	Bagworth	—	—	
Moon, John	Bagworth	—	—	
Roberts, John	Bagworth	—	—	
Wood, Richard	Bagworth	—	—	
Harrison, William	Bagworth park	—	—	
Kirkman, Thomas	Bagworth	—	—	

PARISH OR TOWNSHIP OF BARDON PARK.

NAME:	RESIDENCE.	CURZON	PELL	PAGET
Bacon, Samuel	Newtown Linford	—	—	
Biddle, John	Bardon park	—	—	
Bowley, Joseph	Bardon park	—	—	
Harris, Arthur	Bardon park	—	—	
Harris, Edward	Bardon park	—	—	
Herrick, William Perry	Beaumanor	—	—	
Pickering, William	Bardon park	—	—	
Mollison, William	Bardon park	—	—	
Simpson, Matthew	Bardon park	—	—	
Taylor, Robert	Bardon park	—	—	
Walker, Reuben	Bardon park	—	—	

105, 106 Poll books were introduced in 1696 in order to ensure that returning officers conducted elections more impartially. They continued to be published until the secret ballot was introduced in 1872. Poll books were not necessarily published for every election, but only on demand. The returning officer was only obliged to produce a written copy; the printing was a matter for private enterprise. This poll book of 1719 was produced by Tories disgruntled at their defeat and attempting to show that the sheriff had falsified the poll. The poll book of 1868 was the last issued for a general election.

◄ **104** The Kentish Election of 1734. Although this election was contested with unusual keenness the scene is orderly. Note the open voting, with the clerks entering the votes in the poll books. The voters sport their candidates' favours in their hats. In this election Dering, a Tory, and Vane, a Whig, stood for the 'country interest' against Middlesex and Oxenden, the 'court' candidates. The 'country interest' was able to exploit resentment against Walpole's Excise and local feeling against Middlesex's father, the Duke of Dorset, whose influence in the county was already thought too great by many of the gentry. The parson leads a body of 'court' voters, some of whom are excisemen carrying their staffs of office and books of rates.

107 Hogarth's set of election prints, issued in 1775, satirises the seamy side of politics. *Above: Polling at the Hustings* expresses the artist's disgust at the excesses of party conflict. The halt, lame and blind are being polled. A disabled veteran lays his hook on the bible to take the oath required of each voter (as shown in the poll book of 1719, plate 105), while the lawyers dispute whether the hook fulfils the requirements of the law. Behind, a slobbering idiot in a chair is prompted by a man in irons: this is the demagogue Dr Shebbeare, who had been imprisoned for libelling the king. In the background an election procession crosses a bridge. Below it, Britannia's coach breaks down, while the coachmen play cards on the box.

108 *Chairing the Members* illustrates the disorders that accompany the triumphal procession of the victors. The member in the chair is said to represent Bubb Doddington, one of the greatest borough-mongers of the day. His colleague appears only as a shadow on the wall at the back.

John Wilkes Esqr.

Drawn from the Life and Etch'd in Aquafortis by Will.m Hogarth.

109 Hogarth's penetrating caricature of John Wilkes, drawn in 1763, introduces the theme of radicalism and demagogy that began to disturb the harmony of politics after the accession of George III. Wilkes made his name as a champion of popular liberties when the Secretary of State tried to suppress his paper, the *North Briton*, and the courts declared the attempt illegal. Hogarth shows Wilkes holding the staff and cap of liberty, but with an expression of malevolent cunning and impudence that betrays his true motives. On the table are two numbers of the *North Briton*; No. 45, the subject of the *cause célèbre*, and No. 17, in which Wilkes had attacked Hogarth.

WESTMINSTER ELECTION. 1780.

110 The Westminster Election, 1780. Westminster, with its radical electorate, was a centre of the reform movement aroused by the treatment of Wilkes and America. In this sharp contest Charles James Fox and Admiral Rodney were the successful reform candidates. Fox holds Magna Carta and Rodney a scroll celebrating his victories. A devil flies over the head of the defeated ministerialist. In front Fox's supporters include butchers playing on marrow bones and cleavers and wearing fox's tails in their hats.

111 *The State Quack*, 1762. The licence of political satirists reached extremes in their lampoons on George III's minister Bute. He is depicted performing a play called 'The Senate a Farce'. The tightrope-walker is the king's mother: her performance with the boot is a coarse allusion to her supposed relationship with the minister. The banner showing a Scotsman embracing a woman makes the same point. Satirists made particular play of the fact that Bute was a Scot. In the foreground a Scotsman and a Frenchman exchange greetings: Bute was accused of betraying English interests to the 'auld alliance' between France and Scotland.

The State QUACK

112 *The Political Banditti assailing the Saviour of India*, 1786. Gillray drew this cartoon when Warren Hastings was about to undergo his prolonged impeachment for alleged crimes in the service of the East India Company. His accusers are shown as bandits: Burke on the left, Lord North and, on the right, Fox. The alliance of North and Fox was widely regarded as infamous because they had taken opposite sides over the American colonies. The short-lived coalition government they had formed in 1783 had seemed inspired by greed for power and gain; their abortive bill to regulate the East India Company was condemned as a device to give jobs to their friends. Gillray attributes their pursuit of Hastings to similar sinister motives.

The POLITICAL BANDITTI assailing the SAVIOUR of INDIA.

MASTER BILLY'S PROCESSION TO GROCERS HALL.

113 In *Master Billy's Procession* Rowlandson burlesques the younger Pitt's procession to the City in 1784 to dine with the Grocers' Company and receive the freedom of the City. At front is carried the gold box voted to Pitt. Wilkes, tamed by age and the Gordon riots into supporting authority, carries a banner inscribed 45. Pitt—prime minister at the age of 24—is shown as Master Billy riding in a glorified baby carriage. This support given him by the City was important, for he was still in a minority in the Commons and could only count on the king and Lords. The rough handling he received on returning from the City helped to sway opinion in his favour.

114 *Two Pair of Candidates proposed to the Independant Electors of Middlesex, 1802.* The victory of Pitt in the election of 1784 and the outbreak of the French Revolution put back the cause of parliamentary reform for half a century. But the cause was kept alive, particularly in constituencies like Middlesex with a pronounced radical tradition. This print shows the hustings at Brentford. The reform candidates Byng and Burdett are on the left. Their opponents had opposed an inquiry instigated by Burdett into the management of Cold Bath Prison—the Bastille referred to here. The election was the hottest since the days of Wilkes. Burdett only won his seat because he persuaded the sheriffs to poll 370 owners of two-guinea shares in an uncompleted mill as 40s. freeholders. The result was afterwards reversed.

115, 116 Three 'pocket' boroughs, all disfranchised in 1832. *Above:* Old Sarum, uninhabited in the eighteenth century, still returned two members to Parliament. Voting rights were vested in a bailiff and six burgesses, nominated by the lord of the borough. From 1710 elections were controlled by the Pitt family. This view shows the site of the castle and old cathedral. The field in which elections took place lay to the left, between the mound and the river Avon. *Below:* The twin towns of East and West Looe each returned two members since the sixteenth century. East Looe had some fifty electors. In West Looe the electorate consisted of the corporation, recruited by co-option. Both boroughs were under the patronage of the same family. In 1801 East Looe had 467 and West Looe 376 inhabitants.

117 A borough owner. This is the monument at Weobley, Herefordshire, to Colonel John Birch, who died in 1691. Birch was a self-made man who achieved a command in the parliamentary armies in the Civil War. He was also a good man of business and amassed enough to buy Weobley, among other properties. Having bought the property, he had in effect also bought the parliamentary representation. As the inscription records he sat himself for the borough in the last year of his life.

M. S.
D. JOHANNIS HOLT EQVITIS AVR.
TOTIVS ANGLIÆ IN BANCO REGIO
PER XXI ANNOS CONTINVOS
CAPITALIS IVSTITIARII
GUILIELMO REGI ANNÆQVE REGINÆ
CONSILIARII PERPETVI
LIBERTATIS AC LEGVM ANGLICARVM
ASSERTORIS VINDICIS CVSTODIS
VIGILIS ACRIS ET INTREPIDI
ROLANDVS FRATER VNICVS ET HÆRES
OPTIME DE Æ MERITO
POSUIT.
DIE MARTII Vᵗᵃ A͂C. MDCCIX SVBLATVS EST EX OCVLIS NOSTRIS.
NATVS XXXᵐᵒ DECEMBRIS ANNO MDCXLII.

119 The effigy of Sir Edward Ward at Stoke Doyle, Northants. Ward, who died in 1714, was made Chief Baron of the Exchequer in 1695. Note the careful rendering of the judge's robes and chain of office.

118 The monument of Chief Justice Holt at Redgrave, Suffolk, reflects the majesty that the law had now achieved. Holt, who died in 1710, did much himself to foster the spirit of dignity and independence that characterised the courts in the eighteenth century. His conduct as Chief Justice of the King's Bench was far superior to that of his immediate predecessors, Scroggs and Jeffreys. In the case of *Ashby v White* in 1701 he asserted the rights of the courts even against the House of Commons.

122 A Mayor's court in the early nineteenth century. The Mayor, seen here at his desk, acts in his capacity of justice of the peace. Rowlandson's print, taken from the *Second Tour of Dr Syntax*, shows the doctor's man Pat brought before the court in Bath after coming to blows with some Irish chairmen.

120 *Above left:* A case in progress before the Court of Exchequer at the beginning of the nineteenth century. The Court sat in a room adjoining the north-west corner of Westminster Hall. The judges were the chief baron and three barons of the Exchequer. The cursitor baron, who figures in plate 12, was not a judge: his function in the Court was to administer oaths to sheriffs, bailiffs and officers of the revenue.

121 *Left:* The Court of Arches at Doctors' Commons, 1808. Doctors' Commons, founded in 1511, was an association of practitioners in the civil and canon law. The Court of Arches, chief ecclesiastical court of the province of Canterbury, still exercised jurisdiction over matrimony, divorce, probate and tithe. It lost this jurisdiction in 1857. Doctors' Commons was dissolved the following year. This print shows the Dean of the Arches presiding with the doctors of law. At the table below sit the proctors or solicitors. Note the royal arms, in the central window, and on left and right the symbols of the ecclesiastical and maritime jurisdictions exercised in Doctors' Commons.

BRITANNIA Excifa:

Britain Excis'd.

FOLKS talk of Supplies
To be rais'd by *Excife*,
Old *CALEB* is bloodily nettl'd;
Sure *B——* has more Senfe,
Than to levy new Pence,
Or Troops, when his Peace is quite fettl'd.
Horfe, Foot, and Dragoons,
Battalions, Platoons,
Excife, Wooden Shoes, and no Jury;
Then Taxes increafing,
While Traffick is ceafing,
Would put all the Land in a Fury.

II.

From whence I conclude,
This is wrong underftood,
From his Cradle *B——* hated Oppreffion,
And our King Good and Great
Would have us All eat,
Then dread not, good People, next Seffion.
Horfe, Foot, and Dragoons,
Battalions, Platoons, &c.

III.

See this Dragon, EXCISE,
Has Ten Thoufand Eyes,
And Five Thoufand Mouths to devour us,
A Sting and fharp Claws,
With wide-gaping Jaws,
And a Belly as big as a Store-houfe.
Horfe, Foot, and Dragoons,
Battalions, Platoons, &c.

IV.

This Monfter, Plague rot him!
The Pope firft begot him,
From *Rome* to King *Lewis* he went;
From a *Papift* fo true,
What Good can enfue ?
No Wonder he'll make you keep *Lent.*
Horfe, Foot, and Dragoons,
Battalions, Platoons, &c.

V.

From *France* he flew over,
And landed at *Dover,*
To fwill down your Ale and your Beer;
Now he fwears he can't dine,
Without Sugar and Wine ;
Thus he'll plunder you Year after Year,
Horfe, Foot, and Dragoons,
Battalions, Platoons, &c.

VI.

Grant thefe, and the Glutton
Will roar out for Mutton,
Your Beef, Bread and Bacon to boot ;
Your Goofe, Pig, and Pullet,
He'll thruft down his Gullet,
Whilft the Labourer munches a Root.
Horfe, Foot, and Dragoons,
Battalions, Platoons, &c.

VII.

Befides, 'tis decreed,
The Monfter muft feed,

123, Two sources of revenue. *Above:* Samuel Scott's
124 painting of *The Custom House Quay* shows a
characteristic scene with a customs officer examining merchandise. After the customs ceased to be
farmed out in 1671, their administration became
one of the largest branches of the government service. As the number of revenue officers increased
ministers put their patronage to political use. Some
attempts were made to check this source of
corruption. Customs officers were excluded from
sitting in Parliament and in 1782 Crewe's Act disfranchised them. *Left: Britannia Excisa* was one
of the many virulent attacks made on Walpole's
abortive Excise Bill of 1733. As a tax on domestic
commodities the excise had been introduced in the
Civil War and continued with modification at the
Restoration; with the customs it became the chief
source of the crown's hereditary revenues. It was
always bitterly resented. It evidently increased
prices. It required a body of professional enforcement officers with rights of search and was regarded as an alien, despotic device—a view
reflected in Dr Johnson's famous definition of
excise in his dictionary. Walpole's Bill was a
sensible measure designed to reduce smuggling, but
the name excise aroused every prejudice. It is here
shown as a dragon devouring goods of every sort
and spewing out a stream of money into Walpole's
lap.

Farewell Johnny — Remember me.

Yes D—n thee,—I have reason to remember thee,—but good bye, so thou'rt off. I dont care —go where thou wilt.. thou'lt be a plague to the Land thou lightest on.

IOHN BULL and his FAMILY taking leave of the INCOME TAX

London Pub⁴ by P. Roberts 28 Middle Tow Holborn.

125 The first successful income tax in the world was introduced by Pitt in 1799 as a temporary measure to finance the French war. This cartoon celebrates its repeal in 1802 after the peace of Amiens. It was restored in 1803 and repealed again in 1816. The reduction in the customs made it necessary to re-introduce income tax in 1842; with the achievement of free trade after 1860 it became more or less permanent.

126 The formalities of government must be observed in small things as well as great. *Right:* A justice's order to put in the stocks for the non-payment of 5s. poor rate. For a late instance of the use of the stocks see plate 67.

127 An indenture for drums borrowed by Handel.

His Indenture made the *Twenty Sixth* Day of *Feby 1749* in the *Twenty Third* Year of the Reign of our Sovereign Lord GEORGE the Second, by the Grace of God, King of *Great Britain, France* and *Ireland,* Defender of the Faith, &c. Between *the R¹ Hon.ble the Lieut General Master General* of His MAJESTY's Ordnance, and the Principal Officers of the same, on the Behalf of the KING's most Excellent MAJESTY on the one Part; And *George Frederick Handell Esq.* on the other Part; Witnesseth, That the said *George Frederick Handell* hath received out of His MAJESTY's Stores, within the Office of Ordnance, *at the Tower the Train Kettle Drums undermentioned, the same being directed to be lent him for use of the Oratorio's and to be returned when the same is ended, By Order of the Board dated the 13th Inst*

128 The steady administrative expansion of the eighteenth century, particularly in the revenue and naval departments, made new public buildings necessary. The most impressive of these was Somerset House, begun in 1774. It housed chiefly the Navy and Victualling Offices, but room was found below for the Stamp Office, shown in this print. Stamp duties on paper, vellum and parchment were introduced in 1694 and widely developed afterwards. In the nineteenth century they hindered the development of the popular press, but were not removed from newspapers until 1860 (see plate 193). This picture shows the room in which the papers were stamped. At this time a staff of 80 stampers was required.

129 The Great Reform Bill of 1832. The moment at which the Bill became law: the Royal Assent given by Commission. This painting shows the Commissioners seated in the House of Lords. Brougham, the Lord Chancellor, wearing a black three-cornered hat, presides. The Bill lies on the table, with part falling over the dispatch box to the floor. The Tory benches are empty in protest, their leaders having agreed not to oppose the Bill only because they knew that the King was pledged, if it was defeated, to swamp the House by a wholesale creation of new peers.

130 J. and C. Dodd's *View of Tonbridge during an Election* shows the enthusiasm that was mobilised for the Bill even in a quiet country town. The passing of the Bill was a striking victory for the popular agitation organised by political unions and associations to bring pressure on the government and House of Lords.

131 Many people feared that the reformed House of Commons would be rowdy and irresponsible. The Duke of Wellington is said to have remarked that he had never seen so many bad hats in his life. This engraving by William Heath illustrates these fears: in fact they were groundless.

132 Many radicals feared—with reason—that the new electorate would be corrupted like the old. *Soliciting a Vote*, by R. W. Buss, 1834, shows an educated artisan, who reads political economy and the *Penny Magazine*, being canvassed by Gullem. Gullem's agent prepares to enter the elector's name in his book, while a supporter puts his hand in his pocket, perhaps indicating a bribe.

133 This illustration from an Anti-Corn Law Almanack of 1844 suggests the sort of pressures to which the supposedly independent county elector was exposed. It is a characteristic example of the propaganda lavishly distributed by the Anti-Corn Law League in its attempt to secure the repeal of the protective duties on corn. The League, which was founded in 1839 and achieved its aim in 1846, was an even more successful essay in the mobilisation of national opinion than the political unions that had agitated for the Reform Bill: it anticipated many of the methods used by political parties after 1867. Its temper was relentlessly hostile to the aristocracy and revealed a class antagonism that tended to die down after the middle of the century.

A REAL INDEPENDENT ELECTOR!

(Landlord Stonyheart comes to his Scotch tenant, Donald Mac Dougal, to ask his vote at the coming election for his friend Lord Donegammon. Donald gravely brings out his lease.)—He says,—Well, Donald, what are you looking for?

Donald.—I'm just scanning owr my lease. I dinna ken that thear is ony stipulation aboot ma vote; but if it is in the lease that I must vote as you deseer, I'm a man of my word, and I'll e'en do as I engaged to do in black and white.—*(Reads his lease.)*

Landlord.—Toot! Donald, my good fellow, I don't mean to say that there is a direct agreement, but here it is usual for tenants to do as their landlords wish.

Donald.—The land I till is yours, Mr. Stonyheart, and what rent I agreed for I give. My vote is my own; and, with the blessing of Heaven, I will not give that vote for a man who makes food scarce and dear, to raise rents, and who upholds——

Landlord.—Come, don't din my ears with Anti-Corn-Law stud. Will you vote for Lord Donegammon, the farmers' friend?

Donald.—I must respectfully decline. I, as a farmer, cannot benefit by the ruin of my customers and the——

Landlord.—Ah, well—never mind. Good morning, Sir—good morning.—*(Puts on his hat and flings himself out in a rage.)*—I'll think of you another day.—*(To himself.)*—The tenants-at-will are the men for me.

134 Aristocratic influence also survived in boroughs. Stamford remained under the patronage of the Cecil family. This is a handbill issued by Lord Robert Cecil, later third Marquis of Salisbury, in his first election contest. He represented Stamford until 1868, when he entered the House of Lords.

TO THE
ELECTORS
OF THE
BOROUGH OF STAMFORD.

GENTLEMEN,

Having now completed my Canvass, I take the earliest opportunity of announcing to my friends that the result has been most satisfactory; I therefore request that you will accept my best thanks for the kind and gratifying manner in which I have been received.

As the Election is fixed for Monday next at 10 o'clock precisely, I earnestly request the attendance of my Friends at the George Hotel, Saint Martin's, on that morning, at Half-past 9 o'clock, to accompany me from thence to the Hustings.

I have the honor to be, Gentlemen,

Your obliged and faithful Servant,

ROBERT G. CECIL.

GEORGE HOTEL, Thursday, 18th August, 1853.

H. JOHNSON, PRINTER, ST. MARY'S-HILL, STAMFORD.

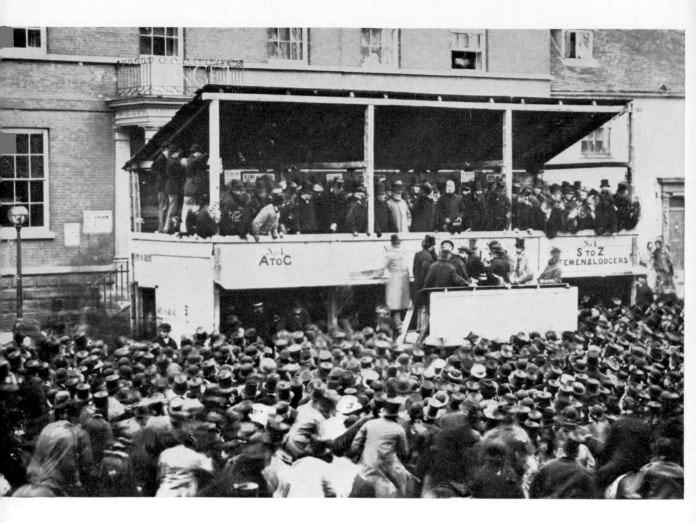

135 The last of the old hustings: the general election at Bury St Edmunds, 1868. Compare the scene at the Kentish election of 1734 (plate 104). Note the reference to the lodgers' franchise, introduced in 1867. After 1872 the introduction of the ballot transformed the ancient procedure.

36, 137 Vote by Ballot. *Above:* The Taunton by-election, 1873, one of the first at which the ballot was used. *Right:* The General Election, Feb. 1874, the first held under the provisions of the Ballot Act. Tenniel's cartoon welcomes the speed of the new procedure and absence of corruption. The ballot deterred corruption because its secrecy made it impossible to ensure a corrupted elector would vote as he was paid to do; but corrupt practices were not eliminated and the first effective Act against them was not passed until 1883.

DEGENERATE DAYS!!

Publican.—*"Call this a General Election? Why, it's all over in about a fortnight, and——"*
Free and Independent Voter.—*"And not a fi-pun-note among 'em."*

THE TWO PATRIOTIC DUCHESS'S ON THEIR CANVASS. 1784
Requesting the favour of an early Poll.

138 Influence and corruption of the old sort may have been eradicated, but certain forms of canvassing remain a permanent part of the electoral scene. Rowlandson's print shows a notorious canvass in the Westminster election of 1784. In support of Fox the beautiful Duchesses of Devonshire and Portland bartered their kisses for votes. Fox won.

139 A liberal candidate, A. W. Yeo, in the Poplar by-election of 1914 makes a fuss of the babies.

140 The extension of the franchise made new techniques of electioneering necessary. Gladstone leaves West Calder during his great Midlothian campaign, Dec. 1879, in which he astonished contemporaries not only by his flow of oratory but by his mobility. The queen was shocked to find a great political leader touring the country like any stump-orator. Note the welcome organised for Gladstone, with festoons, garlands, triumphal arches and inscribed mottoes. The railway had now become a useful aid to electioneering.

141 Sir John Simon conducts an open-air meeting on a building site at Walthamstow, Oct. 1910. A cameraman and reporter are in attendance, they too, represent new techniques of electioneering.

142 Although—or perhaps because—in 1792 Mary Wollstonecraft had championed the cause of Women's Suffrage in *A Vindication of the Rights of Woman,* and the Chartists had to some extent adopted it, the idea of votes for women was not easy to take seriously. George Cruikshank's skit of 1853 expresses the complacent feeling of male superiority that was characteristic of an age when respectable women were confined to domestic life.

143 The first organised attempts to secure votes for women began in 1865, when R. M. Pankhurst founded the Women's Suffrage Committee in Manchester. Forty years later his widow, Emmeline, adopted a policy of calculated violence. Her militant suffragettes conducted the most extraordinary political campaign the country had yet seen. They tried to coerce the government by sensational acts, legal and illegal. They interrupted meetings, intercepted cabinet ministers, chained themselves to railings, smashed windows, threw bombs and set fire to public buildings; and many suffered frequent imprisonment. This photograph shows suffragettes arrested after a demonstration outside Buckingham Palace in 1910.

144 The violence of the suffragettes, which reached its height in 1913, antagonised Parliament and discredited a cause which had been making some progress. Since 1894 women had been allowed to sit on parish and district councils, and on county and borough councils since 1907. The war put an end to agitation and gave women the chance of showing that they could take over many of the responsibilities hitherto reserved to men. In 1918 the Representation of the People Act gave the vote to married women, women householders and university graduates of 30 years of age or more. Another Act of the same year enabled women to sit in the House of Commons. This photograph shows one of the first woman voters, Dec. 1918. The polling clerk is also a woman.

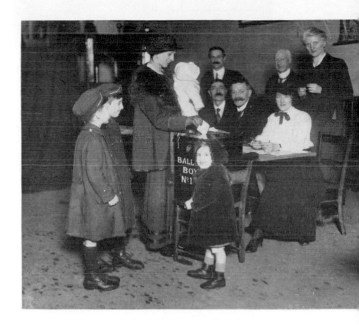

145 Women achieved electoral equality with men in 1929. Here four 'flappers' leave a polling station after voting for the first time. In some countries women had received the vote earlier: they had it in New Zealand in 1893, in Australia in 1902. In the U.S.A. they won it for presidential elections in 1920. They did not have it in France until 1944, in Italy until 1945. They still do not have it in Switzerland.

146 Many of the nineteenth-century reforms in administration, local government, law and penalties were inspired by Jeremy Bentham (1748–1832), founder of English Utilitarianism, and his followers. Bentham maintained that government was a matter of science and the scientific collection and assessment of evidence a necessary prelude to legislation: government must be based on statistics. The census, introduced in 1801 under the supervision of John Rickman, the statistician, was the first step in this direction. The age of the economists and calculators had arrived. This illustration is taken from the census of 1841, the first to provide lists of names.

147 The Union workhouse, Northleach, Gloucestershire. The Poor Law of 1834, described as 'the first great piece of legislation based upon scientific or economical principles', introduced control by a central Board of Commissioners and grouped parishes into new administrative areas, the Poor Law Unions. Relief was to be provided only in the Union workhouse and in conditions calculated to make life in the workhouse substantially less 'eligible' or pleasant than that of the ordinary labourer.

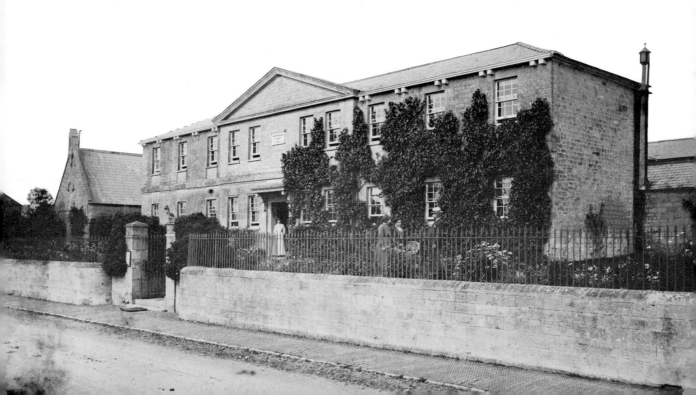

148 Although the new Poor Law introduced central control it maintained the tradition of local responsibility. For the purposes of poor relief the functions of parish vestries and justices of the peace were transferred to elected Boards of Guardians. This engraving of G. B. O'Neill's painting, *The Foundling*, 1852, shows the Guardians determining the future of an abandoned infant. The Boards of Guardians were abolished and administration of the Poor Law was handed over to county councils and boroughs in 1929 and to the Unemployment Assistance Board in 1934.

149 The 'Welfare State' has comprehensively extended the community's responsibility for the unfortunate and handicapped, but abandoned the Poor Law's tendency to treat them as semi-criminal. Old age pensions (1908) and national insurance (1911) narrowed the scope of the Poor Law; and in 1948 the National Assistance Act declared: 'the existing poor law shall cease to have effect'. The workhouse system was abandoned. Before this the Family Allowances Act of 1945 had tackled one of the causes of poverty—that wages bear no relation to the size of family the wage-earner has to support. It entitled parents to receive 5s. a week for the second and every subsequent child under school-leaving age. This photograph shows a mother drawing the first allowance at Vicarage Lane Post Office, Stratford, London.

150 The first Board School erected under the provisions of the Education Act of 1870: Mount Charles Elementary Schools, St Austell, Cornwall. Designed by Sylvanus Trevail, it was opened in Dec. 1872. It accommodated 365 children: the building, furniture and fittings cost about £940. It was described as 'intentionally plain, but very substantial and convenient'.

151 A penny dinner given to Board School children, 1885. The provision of school meals was at first entirely a matter of voluntary initiative. It received official support in 1906, when an act, introduced by a private member, permitted local authorities to provide facilities for these voluntary associations and spend as much as a ½d. rate in their support. Subsequent legislation enlarged these powers until the Education Act of 1944 established the present schools-meals service.

152 Eltham Green Comprehensive School, London, 1956, reflects the scale of the educational expansion initiated by the Act of 1944. In raising the school-leaving age to 15 the Act left open the means by which secondary education would be organised. The policy of the Ministry of Education was to establish a tripartite division into grammar, technical and secondary modern schools. Some local authorities preferred undivided or 'comprehensive' schools; and the L.C.C. adopted this plan in 1947.

soit baillé aux Seigneurs
A ceste bille avecque des
amendemens les Seigneurs
sont assentus.
A ces Amendemens avecque une Amendements
les Communes sont assentus

A N
A C T
TO

Establish public ownership and control of the coal-mining
industry and certain allied activities ; and for purposes
connected therewith.

A.D. 1946.
—

BE it enacted by the King's most Excellent Majesty, by and
with the advice and consent of the Lords Spiritual and
Temporal, and Commons, in this present Parliament assembled,
and by the authority of the same, as follows :—

153 The Bill for the Nationalisation of the Coal Mines, 1946. Note the traditional Norman-French formulae with which the Bill and its amendments were passed from House to House. This represents a stage before the Royal Assent had been given.

154 One purpose of the nationalisation of the mines was to make possible a more rational and efficient exploitation of coal resources. The National Coal Board's installations at Cwm, Glamorgan, illustrate this policy. On the left is the coking and by-product plant, on the right the coal preparation plant and surface buildings of the colliery.

155 A Bow Street runner, one of the body of paid police, the first professional force in England, organised by Henry Fielding, the novelist, after his appointment as a stipendiary magistrate in 1748, with his court at Bow Street. The term 'runner' was normally used for a justice's officer.

156 The last of the old 'Charleys' or night watchmen, photographed outside his box in the Brixton road, London, in the middle of the last century. With the parish constables the 'Charleys' constituted the police force of English towns until 1835. In London they were practically superseded by the Peelers in 1829.

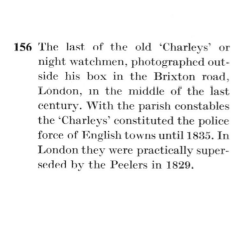

157 *The Law's Delay. Reading the Riot Act*, 1820, by George Cruikshank. Procedure in time of riot had been clarified by the Riot Act of 1715. Hitherto it was not certain with what offence rioters might be charged: sometimes it was treason; and the law did not effectively protect those who suppressed riot. The Act provided that if twelve or more persons, riotously assembled, did not disperse within an hour of a magistrate's reading of the proclamation contained in the Act, they would be guilty of felony; and it indemnified those who dispersed the riot. This procedure helped to distinguish between lawful and unlawful assemblies; but magistrates came to believe that they could not call in the military until they had read the proclamation and waited an hour. Riots could therefore get out of hand, as happened in the Gordon Riots of 1780.

158 Troops entering Euston station to be sent by rail to Birmingham during the Chartist disturbances, 1842. The introduction of the police, some of whom can be seen in action in this engraving, made it less necessary to call on the military to keep public order; but exceptional occasions, like this, still required them. The railways served the cause of order by increasing mobility. These troops had already come by train from Portsmouth.

159 Fascist riot, 1936. Police dismantle a barricade erected by demonstrators near Mark Lane, East London. Beyond it is an overturned lorry.

160 Tenniel's cartoon *The New Medea* sums up the purposes of the Judicature Act, introduced by Lord Selborne, the Lord Chancellor, in 1873. *Punch* commented: 'Lord Selborne is a Medea in a new light. He takes the two ugly little children—Law and Equity—and tosses them into a cauldron, wherein he proposes to fuse them, and to bring out a perfect Angel of Light.'

161 The Central Criminal Court at the Old Bailey, 1880. It was established in 1834 as the court of assize for the criminal business of London, Middlesex and some parts of the home counties. The trial is that of the German anarchist Johann Most, editor of *Freiheit*, a revolutionary weekly. His counsel is the celebrated Irish barrister A. M. Sullivan. Most, who had already been expelled from Germany, later settled in the U.S.A. after serving a prison sentence here.

THE NEW MEDEA.

Jason (Mr. Bull).—" *Goodness gracious !*—(*Aside*)—*I hope it's all right—but there'll be an awful row !*

162 The lock-up on the bridge at Bradford-on-Avon, Wilts., was probably built in the seventeenth century and served its purpose until the erection of the Town Hall in 1855. It may also have acted as a toll-house.

163 Rowlandson's print of the King's Bench Prison shows the free and easy conditions that still prevailed in some prisons at the opening of the nineteenth century. It was a place of confinement for debtors and for those sentenced by the Court of King's Bench for libels and other misdemeanours. It was possible for prisoners to buy the freedom to walk in St. George's Fields outside.

164 The Surrey House of Correction, Wandsworth, opened in 1851, was one of the new prisons built on the model of Pentonville, ten years its senior. Its discipline was based on the 'separate' system, under which the prisoners were isolated from one another as much as possible. They were housed in large blocks of single cells, in which they ate, worked and slept. At exercise they wore masks to prevent recognition. Most of our existing prisons were built at this time and on this plan.

165 The Prison Chapel, Pentonville, about 1850. Here and at some other prisons the principle of separation was taken to extreme lengths. Even in chapel the prisoners were prevented from seeing each other by wooden partitions which allowed them only to look to their front. The partitions were hinged like doors for entrance and exit. A good example of this arrangement may be seen by the public in the old prison within Lincoln Castle.

166 The Borstal, Portland. The establishment of special training centres for youthful offenders was one of the first consequences of the Gladstone Report of 1895, which recommended that the mid-Victorian concentration on deterrence and punishment should give place to reformation and training and that special categories of offenders, particularly the young, should have special treatment. The first was set up in 1902 and occupied Rochester Prison, which stands in the village of Borstal. As this photograph shows, the Portland Borstal also suffers the handicap of occupying the grim blocks of a Victorian prison. Since 1930 experiments have been made with open Borstals. Borstal training is provided for offenders between the ages of 16 and 21.

167 Approved Schools provide for children whom the courts consider to be in need of residential care and protection, usually after methods such as probation have failed. They are approved by the Home Secretary (or the Secretary of State for Scotland), but are provided by local authorities or voluntary organisations. This photograph shows a class in a Salvation Army Approved School.

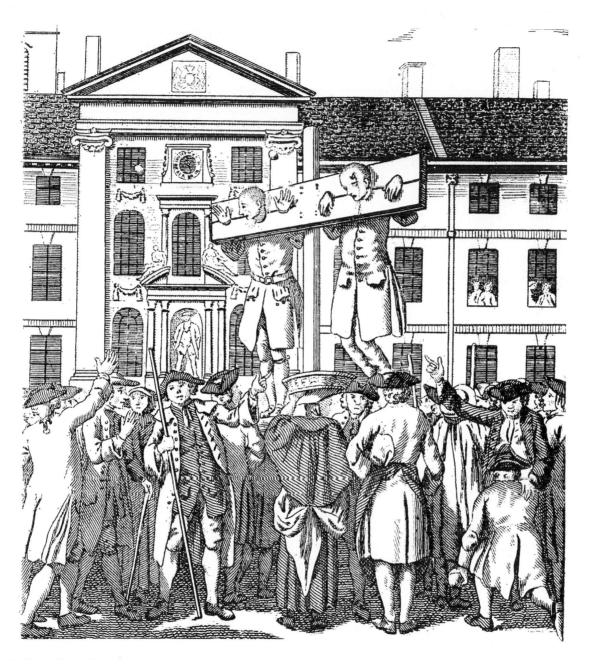

168 The pillory, like the stocks, was a familiar feature of town and village before imprisonment was introduced as a punishment rather than temporary restraint. Its purpose was public humiliation; but its effect was arbitrary. The victim might be pelted with offensive but harmless rubbish; or he might be stoned to death, as happened to Egan the thieftaker at Smithfield, shown in this print from the Newgate Calendar. The pillory was last used in London in 1830: the penalty was abolished in 1837.

Mode of punishment by **BRANDING**, *or burning on the* **HAND**, *at the New Sessions House.*

169 Branding was another form of humiliation, usually employed as an additional penalty. The criminal was branded on the face or hand with the initial letter of his crime, such as V for vagrancy; the most common mark was M for malefactor. The penalty was abolished in the middle of the eighteenth century.

170 The *peine forte et dure*, or pressing with weights, the only torture the Common Law recognised, was used not to extract evidence but to enable a trial to begin by forcing the accused to plead. Some persons, unlike William Spiggot here, died rather than risk conviction and penalties that might harm their dependants. It was last inflicted at the Cambridge Assizes in 1741. Refusal to plead was treated after 1772 as a plea of guilty, after 1827 as a plea of not guilty.

171 This watercolour of 1823 by H. Goddard shows the treadmill at the borough gaol, Highcross Street, Leicester. The treadmill was one of the devices advocated by prison reformers to make prison more of a deterrent. In some prisons treadmills were used for useful purposes, such as grinding grain or pumping water. In most the labour was quite useless, the necessary resistance being provided by large vanes which turned purposelessly in the air. Advocates of the separate system found the treadmill too sociable: they preferred to set prisoners to do 12,000 revolutions a day on crank machines placed in isolated cells.

172 Transportation was introduced as an alternative to the death penalty for serious offences in the seventeenth century, when overseas territories first became available. It provided a convenient means of ridding society of delinquents and colonising empty lands such as Australia, which became the chief destination of transported convicts after the American colonies had been lost. After Australian protests the Penal Servitude Acts of 1853 and 1857 put an end to transportation and replaced it by the prison system. This engraving shows convicts caged in a transport ship not long before the abolition.

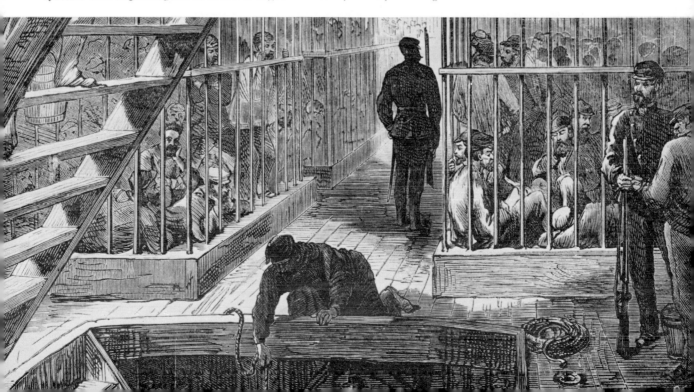

173 Inspection of weights and measures is one of the oldest functions of local government. Here a L.C.C. coal officer watches while a coalman heaves a sack on the scales.

174 The march of the Poplar Borough Council to prison, September 1921. As this was a time of severe unemployment and the cost of poor relief still had to be met locally, the hardest hit areas were saddled with crippling bills while many wealthy areas were unaffected. The contrast was particularly striking in London. To draw attention to the injustice Poplar Council refused to pay and were committed to prison. Six weeks later a temporary Act shifted part of the burden; but no permanent change was achieved until the Acts of 1929 and 1934. Note George Lansbury, then Mayor of Poplar, carrying a coat over his left shoulder.

175 The Queen Elizabeth Hospital, Birmingham, opened in 1938, illustrates local initiative in social policy. After 1873, when Joseph Chamberlain became Mayor, Birmingham adopted a policy of municipal service that set a standard for the rest of the country. This hospital originated in the corporation's resolution of 1924 to secure a co-ordinated scheme for hospital development. The Birmingham Hospitals Council, a voluntary organisation, supported by the corporation and massive private subscriptions, then developed the plan which fructified in 1938 and anticipated methods later adopted by the National Health Service.

176 The Museums Committee of Norwich City Council, 1952. In Norwich the first museum was opened by private subscribers in 1825: in 1893 the collection was made over to the corporation. This committee illustrates some features of local government: it is composed partly of councillors, the Lord Mayor occupying the chair; partly of permanent officials, including the then curator Miss Barnard and her deputy the late Mr Clarke (standing by the Lord Mayor), and partly of co-opted members. The committee is seen examining new acquisitions.

177 An old town hall: Leicester Guildhall. This was built for the Corpus Christi gild, an association of townsmen which supported chantry priests in the neighbouring church and performed other devotional services. The Town Council began to meet in the hall towards the end of the fifteenth century and in 1563, after the gild had been dissolved, bought it. It served as the town hall until 1876. The photograph shows the interior of the great hall, constructed in the fifteenth century. It was much used for civic feasts and plays. Edward Alleyn and Richard Burbage certainly played there and possibly Shakespeare.

178 Worcester Guildhall represents the civic magnificence of the eighteenth century. It was designed by Thomas White, completed in 1723. The statues in the niches witness the city's loyalty to the House of Stuart: Queen Anne stands above the door, to the left is Charles I supporting the church, and to the right Charles II supports kingly government. The interior contains courts for assizes and sessions, and a splendid council chamber, rebuilt in 1791, which also served as public assembly rooms.

179 Corfe Town Hall illustrates the variety of municipal government in the eighteenth century. The history of the building is obscure, its architecture undistinguished. It was erected in the second half of the century, probably on a medieval base.

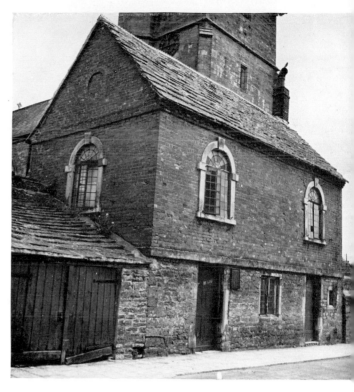

180 Leicester Town Hall under construction, 1874–6. In very many towns the Town Hall is the most impressive monument of Victorian municipal vigour. In Leicester a sense of economy delayed this enterprise with the fortunate result that this accomplished design by F. J. Hames avoided the Gothic exuberance which might have been obligatory ten years earlier.

181 The heart of a capital city: Cardiff. This aerial view of Cathays Park reveals a rare concentration of local and national institutions. The City Hall of 1904 stands in the centre, flanked by the Law Courts (left) and the Welsh National Museum (right), opened in 1927. The University College, founded in 1883, lies behind the museum. Behind the City Hall is the National War Memorial and, beyond, the Welsh Board of Health, opened in 1938. Glamorgan County Hall, the Technical College and the Welsh Regional Hospital Board are behind the Law Courts. In the left foreground is the castle mound and keep, presented to the city by the Marquis of Bute in 1947.

182, Welsh nationalism: a bookshop at the Caernarvon
183 headquarters of the Welsh National Party. The principal object of this party is to obtain a separate Welsh parliament. *Below:* Welsh nationalism in action: a march to protest against the occupation of land in mid-Wales by the War Office. Welsh nationalists are particularly sensitive about the use of Welsh resources for the benefit of their English neighbours. They have protested about the building of waterworks and power stations: extremists have resorted to acts of sabotage.

184 Although Scotland no longer has her own parliament some of her old representative institutions survive. One of these is the General Assembly of the Kirk; another is the Convention of Royal Burghs, shown here meeting in Edinburgh. The origin of the Convention is obscure: its formal existence was recognised in the sixteenth century. Its purpose was to defend the extensive commercial privileges of the royal burghs and to proportion between them their share of national taxation. As new forms of taxation were adopted and their commercial privileges decayed the Convention remained chiefly important as an obstinate opponent of municipal reform. Since 1833 the Convention has been reconstituted and now acts as a useful forum for discussing the mutual interests of the Scottish municipalities.

185 The Scottish Covenant of 1950. In recent years Scottish nationalists have tried to rally public support for a programme transcending ordinary party differences and concentrating on the demand for a separate Scottish parliament. The Covenant, in which this demand is expressed and which the public are asked to sign, harks back to the famous National Covenant of 1638.

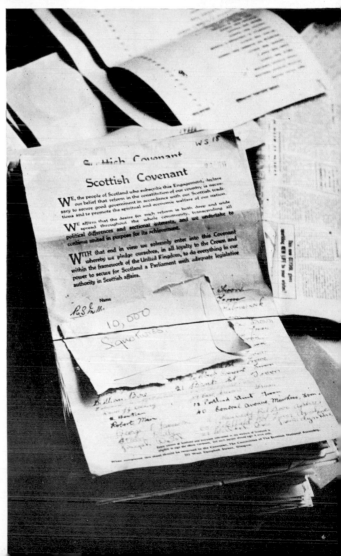

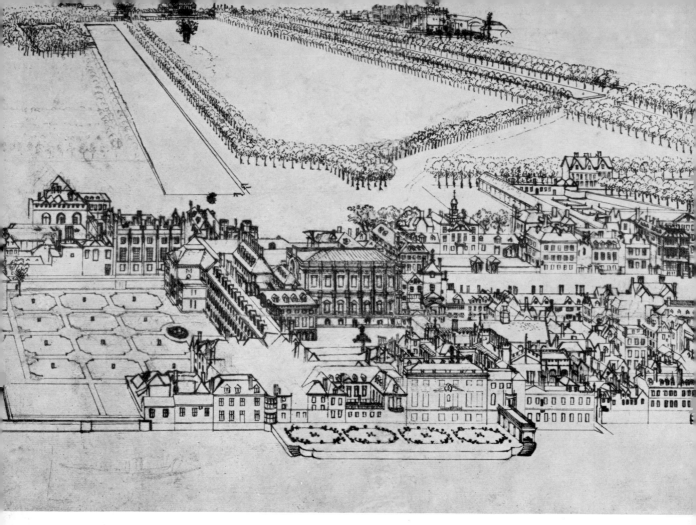

186 A bird's eye view of Whitehall, about 1696. Westminster, home of Parliament and (formerly) the courts, was the creation of the medieval kings. Whitehall, as the centre of executive government, was the creation of the Tudors and Stuarts. Like Westminster, Whitehall began as a royal palace, erected after 1529 when Henry VIII took possession of Wolsey's York Place. At the time Knyff made this drawing the palace contained over 2,000 rooms. In the foreground the view shows the landing stairs and queen's apartments. Behind them is the Banqueting Hall, with the Horse Guards and Admiralty buildings to its right, across the road. The turrets of the Holbein gate, which obstructed the road, can be seen just behind and to the left of the Banqueting Hall. The privy garden occupies the left foreground and among the buildings behind it is the Cockpit, important because it became the permanent home of the Treasury. Whitehall ceased to be a royal residence after a destructive fire in 1698, but remained the centre of administration, which no longer had to follow the king.

187 *Above right:* The Treasury Buildings, 1846. This is only one of the government offices which transformed the appearance of Whitehall and Parliament Street in Victoria's reign. Kent completed a new Treasury on the site of the Cockpit in 1736. A new building had to be added by Soane in 1827; but it soon proved too small and was reconstructed and enlarged by Barry in 1846. It is now undergoing a further reconstruction.

188 *Below:* Whitehall Gardens, the most recent monument of administrative expansion.

189 The Treasury and Downing Street from St James's Park, 1827. J. C. Buckler's drawing shows the deceptively domestic character of the centre of government. Since his time the houses that used to close the end of Downing Street have been removed, but those that remain have kept their unpretentious appearance and secluded gardens. Downing Street received its name from Sir George Downing, who had a large part in the management of the Treasury during Charles II's reign: it was laid out at the end of the reign. The houses belonged to the Treasury; and so Number 10 became available to the Prime Minister in his capacity as First Lord of the Treasury. It has been the permanent official residence of the Prime Minister since 1885.

190 The Cabinet Room, No. 10 Downing Street. It has the modest scale and sober elegance of a gentleman's town house.

191, Three conflicts between Lords and Commons.
192, *Right:* This newspaper stamp recalls the dispute of
193 1860–1, when the Lords rejected Gladstone's repeal of the paper duties. Next year Gladstone put it, with all his financial proposals, into a single budget, which the Lords dared not reject. Tenniel's cartoon *Ajax defying the Lightning* of 1871 celebrated another victory of Gladstone over the Lords after they rejected a bill to abolish the purchase of commissions in the Army. He turned their flank by persuading the queen to abolish Purchase by Royal Warrant. *The Old Trojan*, August 1911. This cartoon illustrates the Lords' opposition to the Parliament Bill. The 'die-hards', led by Lord Halsbury, resolved to reject the Bill and throw on the king the opprobrium of having to carry out his promise to create 300 peers. In a close vote the moderates, led by Lord Lansdowne, just carried the day and the Parliament Bill became law.

AJAX DEFYING THE LIGHTNING.

THE OLD TROJAN.

LORD LANSDOWNE. "DON'T LUG THAT INFERNAL MACHINE INTO THE CITADEL. THE THING'S FULL OF ENEMIES."

LORD HALSBURY. "I KNOW. THAT'S WHERE MY HEROISM COMES IN."

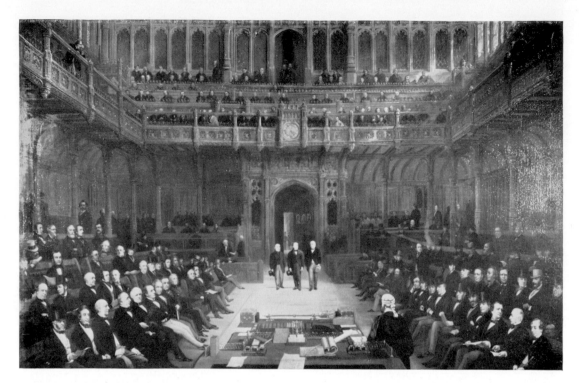

194 *Baron Lionel de Rothschild Introduced into the House of Commons*, 1858. The first Jewish M.P. advances between his 'introducers' to take his seat. The Jewish Relief Act had just allowed the Commons to abandon the oath 'upon the true faith of a Christian' which prevented Jews benefiting from the earlier abolition of religious Tests. Lord John Russell, who took a large part in the struggle, walks on Rothschild's left. Disraeli, a Jew by ancestry but not in religion, sits on the government front bench. The emancipation of the Jews was completed in 1885 when Rothschild's son took his seat in the Lords.

196 The Division Lobby of the House of Commons, 1857. Divisions were rare before the reign of Elizabeth I; and it long remained the practice that, when the House divided, only the Ayes left the chamber. This practice was alleged to favour the Noes, for members were reluctant to risk losing their places. Present procedure requires all members wishing to vote to go into the division lobbies that run down each side of the chamber. After six minutes the entrances to the lobbies are locked and the members file out of the exit doors past the desks, where they are counted. At each lobby there is a clerk, who records the names of the members, and two tellers, one for the Ayes, one for the Noes, who count them aloud.

◀ **195** The Commons Chamber, rebuilt after Barry's and Pugin's work of 1852 had been destroyed in an air raid. It was opened in 1950. The new chamber has the same dimensions as the old and like the old, by a deliberate decision, cannot seat all its members, providing for 437 out of 625. A comparison with the painting above shows how the reconstruction, while preserving the Gothic outline, has bowdlerised the Gothic richness of the old chamber.

COBBETT'S
Parliamentary Debates

DURING THE

SECOND SESSION OF THE FOURTH PARLIAMENT

OF THE

UNITED KINGDOM OF GREAT BRITAIN AND IRELAND,

AND OF THE

KINGDOM OF GREAT BRITAIN THE TWENTY-FIRST,

Appointed to meet at Westminster, the Twenty-first Day of January, in the Forty-eighth Year of the Reign of His Majesty King GEORGE the Third, Annoque Domini One Thousand Eight Hundred and Eight.

VOL. X.

COMPRISING THE PERIOD

BETWEEN THE 21ST OF JAN. AND THE 8TH OF APRIL, 1808.

LONDON:

PRINTED BY T. C. HANSARD, PETERBOROUGH-COURT, FLEET-STREET.

197 Cobbett's *Parliamentary Debates*, the precursor of *Hansard*. This is the first issue on which the name of Hansard appears as printer.

198 Tenniel's cartoon of 1865 reflects on the seclusion into which Queen Victoria withdrew after the Prince Consort's death in 1861. Although she continued to devote herself with customary industry to routine business she completely neglected the public ceremonies of monarchy. For twenty years her public appearances were so rare as to encourage the most outspoken criticism of the monarchy as an institution.

QUEEN HERMIONE.

PAULINA (BRITANNIA) UNVEILS THE STATUE. "'TIS TIME! DESCEND; BE STONE NO MORE!"

199 Queen Victoria's diamond jubilee, 1897: the state procession through London. The queen is sitting in an open landau under a parasol. By this time the coldness of the middle years of the reign had passed and the splendid occasion was marked by unparalleled demonstrations of loyalty.

200 The State Opening of Parliament is one of the most impressive occasions in the calendar of royal ceremonies. This photograph shows Her Majesty leaving Buckingham Palace in the Irish State Coach followed by a detachment of Life Guards.

201 H.M. Queen Elizabeth II with the traditional symbols of her dignity. This photograph was taken by Mr Cecil Beaton, the distinguished photographer, after the coronation, 2 June 1953. Her Majesty wears her coronation dress and purple velvet robe. The crown is the Imperial State Crown, made in 1837: its uppermost cross contains a sapphire that may be the oldest of all the Crown Jewels, reputedly the stone from the ring of Edward the Confessor. The orb is in her left hand and in her right she holds the sceptre with the cross, ensign of kingly power and justice. The golden bracelets or Armills were presented by the Commonwealth countries and were being used for the first time.

Index

The figures in italics refer to the illustrations on page 73 onwards

N

INDEX

INDEX